D1521761

POEMS

BY

WILLIAM CULLEN BRYANT.

COLLECTED AND ARRANGED

BY THE AUTHOR.

IN TWO VOLUMES.

VOL. I.

NEW YORK:

D. APPLETON AND COMPANY.

443 & 445 BROADWAY.

LONDON: 16 LITTLE BRITAIN

M.DCCC.LXII.

811
B

TO THE READER.

[PREFIXED TO THE EDITION OF 1846.]

PERHAPS it would have been well if the author had followed his original intention, which was to leave out of this edition, as unworthy of republication, several of the poems which made a part of his previous collections. He asks leave to plead the judgment of a literary friend, whose opinion in such matters he highly values, as his apology for having retained them. With the exception of the first and longest poem in the collection, "The Ages," they are all arranged according to the order of time in which they were written, as far as it can be ascertained.

New York, 1846.

ADVERTISEMENT.

THE present edition has been carefully revised by the author, and some faults of diction and versification corrected. A few poems not in the previous editions have been added.

New York, August, 1854.

CONTENTS OF VOL. I.

Poems.

POEMS.

POEMS.

THE AGES.

I.

When to the common rest that crowns our days,
Called in the noon of life, the good man goes,
Or full of years, and ripe in wisdom, lays
His silver temples in their last repose ;
When, o'er the buds of youth, the death-wind
      blows,
And blights the fairest ; when our bitter tears
Stream, as the eyes of those that love us close,
We think on what they were, with many fears
Lest goodness die with them, and leave the
      coming years.

II.

And therefore, to our hearts, the days gone by,
When lived the honoured sage whose death we
      wept,
And the soft virtues beamed from many an eye,
And beat in many a heart that long has slept,—
Like spots of earth where angel-feet have
      stepped,
Are holy ; and high-dreaming bards have told
Of times when worth was crowned, and faith
      was kept,
Ere friendship grew a snare, or love waxed cold—
Those pure and happy times—the golden days
      of old.

III.

Peace to the just man's memory ; let it grow
Greener with years, and blossom through the
      flight

Of ages ; let the mimic canvas show
His calm benevolent features ; let the light
Stream on his deeds of love, that shunned the
    sight
Of all but heaven, and, in the book of fame,
The glorious record of his virtues write,
And hold it up to men, and bid them claim
A palm like his, and catch from him the hal-
    lowed flame.

IV.

But oh, despair not of their fate who rise
To dwell upon the earth when we withdraw !
Lo ! the same shaft by which the righteous dies,
Strikes through the wretch that scoffed at
    mercy's law,
And trode his brethren down, and felt no awe
Of Him who will avenge them. Stainless worth,
Such as the sternest age of virtue saw,

Ripens, meanwhile, till time shall call it forth
From the low modest shade, to light and bless
    the earth.

v.

Has Nature, in her calm, majestic march
Faltered with age at last ? does the bright sun
Grow dim in heaven ? or, in their far blue
    arch,
Sparkle the crowd of stars, when day is done,
Less brightly ? when the dew-lipped Spring
    comes on,
Breathes she with airs less soft, or scents the
    sky
With flowers less fair than when her reign be-
    gun ?
Does prodigal Autumn, to our age, deny
The plenty that once swelled beneath his sober
    eye ?

VI.

Look on this beautiful world, and read the truth
In her fair page ; see, every season brings
New change, to her, of everlasting youth ;
Still the green soil, with joyous living things,
Swarms, the wide air is full of joyous wings,
And myriads, still, are happy in the sleep
Of ocean's azure gulfs, and where he flings
The restless surge. Eternal Love doth keep
In his complacent arms, the earth, the air, the
    deep.

VII.

Will then the merciful One, who stamped our
    race
With his own image, and who gave them sway
O'er earth and the glad dwellers on her face,
Now that our swarming nations far away

Are spread, where'er the moist earth drinks the
    day,
Forget the ancient care that taught and nursed
His latest offspring? will he quench the ray
Infused by his own forming smile at first,
And leave a work so fair all blighted and ac-
    cursed?

VIII.

Oh, no! a thousand cheerful omens give
Hope of yet happier days, whose dawn is nigh.
He who has tamed the elements shall not live
The slave of his own passions; he whose eye
Unwinds the eternal dances of the sky,
And in the abyss of brightness dares to span
The sun's broad circle, rising yet more high,
In God's magnificent works his will shall scan—
And love and peace shall make their paradise
    with man.

IX.

Sit at the feet of history—through the night
Of years the steps of virtue she shall trace,
And show the earlier ages, where her sight
Can pierce the eternal shadows o'er their face ;—
When, from the genial cradle of our race,
Went forth the tribes of men, their pleasant lot
To choose, where palm-groves cooled their
      dwelling-place,
Or freshening rivers ran ; and there forgot
The truth of heaven, and kneeled to gods that
      heard them not.

X.

Then waited not the murderer for the night,
But smote his brother down in the bright day,
And he who felt the wrong, and had the might,
His own avenger, girt himself to slay ;
Beside the path the unburied carcass lay ;

The shepherd, by the fountains of the glen,
Fled, while the robber swept his flock away,
And slew his babes.   The sick, untended then,
Languished in the damp shade, and died afar
        from men.

XI.

But misery brought in love—in passion's strife
Man gave his heart to mercy, pleading long,
And sought out gentle deeds to gladden life ;
The weak, against the sons of spoil and wrong,
Banded, and watched their hamlets, and grew
        strong.
States rose, and, in the shadow of their might,
The timid rested.   To the reverent throng,
Grave and time-wrinkled men, with locks all
        white,
Gave laws, and judged their strifes, and taught
        the way of right ;

XII.

Till bolder spirits seized the rule and nailed
On men the yoke that man should never bear,
And drove them forth to battle. Lo ! unveiled
The scene of those stern ages ! What is there !
A boundless sea of blood, and the wild air
Moans with the crimson surges that entomb
Cities and bannered armies ; forms that wear
The kingly circlet rise, amid the gloom,
O'er the dark wave, and straight are swallowed
  in its womb.

XIII.

Those ages have no memory—but they left
A record in the desert—columns strown
On the waste sands, and statues fallen and cleft,
Heaped like a host in battle overthrown ;
Vast ruins, where the mountain's ribs of stone
Were hewn into a city ; streets that spread
 Vol. I.—1*

In the dark earth, where never breath has blown
Of heaven's sweet air, nor foot of man dares tread
The long and perilous ways—the Cities of the
        Dead :

XIV.

And tombs of monarchs to the clouds up-piled—
They perished—but the eternal tombs remain—
And the black precipice, abrupt and wild,
Pierced by long toil and hollowed to a fane ;—
Huge piers and frowning forms of gods sustain
The everlasting arches, dark and wide,
Like the night-heaven, when clouds are black
        with rain.
But idly skill was tasked, and strength was
        plied,
All was the work of slaves to swell a despot's
        pride.

XV.

And Virtue cannot dwell with slaves, nor reign
O'er those who cower to take a tyrant's yoke ;
She left the down-trod nations in disdain,
And flew to Greece, when Liberty awoke,
New-born, amid those glorious vales, and broke
Sceptre and chain with her fair youthful hands:
As rocks are shivered in the thunder-stroke.
And lo ! in full-grown strength, an empire
stands
Of leagued and rival states, the wonder of the
lands.

XVI.

Oh, Greece ! thy flourishing cities were a spoil
Unto each other ; thy hard hand oppressed
And crushed the helpless ; thou didst make thy
soil
Drunk with the blood of those that loved thee
best ;

And thou didst drive, from thy unnatural breast,
Thy just and brave to die in distant climes ;
Earth shuddered at thy deeds, and sighed for
     rest
From thine abominations ; after times,
That yet shall read thy tale, will tremble at
     thy crimes.

XVII.

Yet there was that within thee which has saved
Thy glory, and redeemed thy blotted name ;
The story of thy better deeds, engraved
On fame's unmouldering pillar, puts to shame
Our chiller virtue ; the high art to tame
The whirlwind of the passions was thine own ;
And the pure ray, that from thy bosom came,
Far over many a land and age has shone,
  And mingles with the light that beams from
     God's own throne.

XVIII.

And Rome, thy sterner, younger sister, she
Who awed the world with her imperial frown,
Rome drew the spirit of her race from thee,—
The rival of thy shame and thy renown.
Yet her degenerate children sold the crown
Of earth's wide kingdoms to a line of slaves;
Guilt reigned, and wo with guilt, and plagues came down,
       came down,
Till the north broke its floodgates, and the
       waves
Whelmed the degraded race, and weltered o'er
       their graves.

XIX.

Vainly that ray of brightness from above,
That shone around the Galilean lake,
The light of hope, the leading star of love,
Struggled, the darkness of that day to break;

Even its own faithless guardians strove to
       slake,
In fogs of earth, the pure ethereal flame ;
And priestly hands, for Jesus' blessed sake,
Were red with blood, and charity became,
In that stern war of forms, a mockery and a
       name.

XX.

They triumphed, and less bloody rites were kept
Within the quiet of the convent cell ;
The well-fed inmates pattered prayer, and slept,
And sinned, and liked their easy penance well.
Where pleasant was the spot for men to dwell,
Amid its fair broad lands the abbey lay,
Sheltering dark orgies that were shame to tell,
And cowled and barefoot beggars swarmed the
       way,
All in their convent weeds, of black, and white,
       and gray.

XXI.

Oh, sweetly the returning muses' strain
Swelled over that famed stream, whose gentle
tide
In their bright lap the Etrurian vales detain,
Sweet, as when winter storms have ceased to
chide,
And all the new-leaved woods, resounding wide,
Send out wild hymns upon the scented air.
Lo ! to the smiling Arno's classic side
The emulous nations of the west repair,
And kindle their quenched urns, and drink
fresh spirit there.

XXII.

Still, Heaven deferred the hour ordained to
rend
From saintly rottenness the sacred stole ;
And cowl and worshipped shrine could still
defend

The wretch with felon stains upon his soul ;
And crimes were set to sale, and hard his dole
Who could not bribe a passage to the skies ;
And vice, beneath the mitre's kind control,
Sinned gaily on, and grew to giant size,
Shielded by priestly power, and watched by
     priestly eyes.

XXIII.

At last the earthquake came—the shock, that
     hurled
To dust, in many fragments dashed and strown,
The throne, whose roots were in another world,
And whose far-stretching shadow awed our own.
From many a proud monastic pile, o'erthrown,
Fear-struck, the hooded inmates rushed and fled;
The web, that for a thousand years had grown
O'er prostrate Europe, in that day of dread
Crumbled and fell, as fire dissolves the flaxen
     thread.

XXIV.

The spirit of that day is still awake,
And spreads himself, and shall not sleep again;
But through the idle mesh of power shall break
Like billows o'er the Asian monarch's chain;
Till men are filled with him, and feel how vain,
Instead of the pure heart and innocent hands,
Are all the proud and pompous modes to gain
The smile of heaven;—till a new age expands
Its white and holy wings above the peaceful
    lands.

XXV.

For look again on the past years;—behold,
How like the nightmare's dreams have flown
    away
Horrible forms of worship, that, of old,
Held o'er the shuddering realms, unquestioned
    sway:
See crimes, that feared not once the eye of day,

Rooted from men, without a name or place ,
See nations blotted out from earth, to pay
The forfeit of deep guilt ;—with glad embrace
The fair disburdened lands welcome a nobler
  race.

XXVI.

Thus error's monstrous shapes from earth are
  driven ;
They fade, they fly, but truth survives their
  flight ;
Earth has no shades to quench that beam of
  heaven ;
Each ray that shone, in early time, to light
The faltering footstep in the path of right,
Each gleam of clearer brightness shed to aid
In man's maturer day his bolder sight,
All blended, like the rainbow's radiant braid,
Pour yet, and still shall pour, the blaze that
  cannot fade.

XXVII.

Late, from this western shore, that morning
    chased
The deep and ancient night, which threw its
    shroud
O'er the green land of groves, the beautiful
    waste,
Nurse of full streams, and lifter-up of proud
Sky-mingling mountains that o'erlook the cloud.
Erewhile, where yon gay spires their brightness
    rear,
Trees waved, and the brown hunter's shouts
    were loud
Amid the forest ; and the bounding deer
Fled at the glancing plume, and the gaunt
    wolf yelled near,

XXVIII.

And where his willing waves yon bright blue bay
Sends up, to kiss his decorated brim,

And cradles, in his soft embrace, the gay
Young group of grassy islands born of him,
And crowding nigh, or in the distance dim,
Lifts the white throng of sails, that bear or bring
The commerce of the world ;—with tawny limb,
And belt and beads in sunlight glistening,
The savage urged his skiff like wild bird on the
　　　wing.

XXIX.

Then all this youthful paradise around,
And all the broad and boundless mainland, lay
Cooled by the interminable wood, that frowned
O'er mount and vale, where never summer ray
Glanced, till the strong tornado broke his way
Through the gray giants of the sylvan wild ;
Yet many a sheltered glade, with blossoms gay,
Beneath the showery sky and sunshine mild,
Within the shaggy arms of that dark forest
　　　smiled.

XXX

There stood the Indian hamlet, there the lake
Spread its blue sheet that flashed with many
an oar,
Where the brown otter plunged him from the
brake,
And the deer drank: as the light gale flew o'er,
The twinkling maize-field rustled on the shore;
And while that spot, so wild, and lone, and fair,
A look of glad and guiltless beauty wore,
And peace was on the earth and in the air,
The warrior lit the pile, and bound his captive
there :

XXXI.

Not unavenged ; the foeman, from the wood,
Beheld the deed, and when the midnight shade
Was stillest, gorged his battle-axe with blood ;
All died—the wailing babe—the shrieking maid—

And in the flood of fire that scathed the glade,
The roofs went down; but deep the silence grew,
When on the dewy woods the day-beam played;
No more the cabin smokes rose wreathed and
      blue,
And ever, by their lake, lay moored the bark
      canoe.

XXXII.

Look now abroad—another race has filled
These populous borders—wide the wood recedes,
And towns shoot up, and fertile realms are tilled;
The land is full of harvests and green meads;
Streams numberless, that many a fountain feeds,
Shine, disembowered, and give to sun and
      breeze
Their virgin waters; the full region leads
New colonies forth, that toward the western seas
Spread, like a rapid flame among the autumnal
      trees.

XXXIII.

Here the free spirit of mankind, at length,
Throws its last fetters off ; and who shall place
A limit to the giant's unchained strength,
Or curb his swiftness in the forward race ?
On, like the comet's way through infinite space
Stretches the long untravelled path of light,
Into the depths of ages : we may trace,
Afar, the brightening glory of its flight,
Till the receding rays are lost to human sight.

XXXIV.

Europe is given a prey to sterner fates,
And writhes in shackles ; strong the arms
        that chain
To earth her struggling multitude of states ;
She too is strong, and might not chafe in vain
Against them, but might fling to earth the
        train

That trample her, and break their iron net.
Yes, she shall look on brighter days and gain
The meed of worthier deeds ; the moment set
To rescue and raise up, draws near—but is not
     yet.

XXXV.

But thou, my country, thou shalt never fall,
Save with thy children—thy maternal care,
Thy lavish love, thy blessings showered on all—
These are thy fetters—seas and stormy air
Are the wide barrier of thy borders, where,
Among thy gallant sons that guard thee well,
Thou laugh'st at enemies : who shall then de-
     clare
The date of thy deep-founded strength, or tell
How happy, in thy lap, the sons of men shall
     dwell ?

THANATOPSIS.

To him who in the love of Nature holds
Communion with her visible forms, she speaks
A various language ; for his gayer hours
She has a voice of gladness, and a smile
And eloquence of beauty, and she glides
Into his darker musings, with a mild
And healing sympathy, that steals away
Their sharpness ere he is aware. When thoughts
Of the last bitter hour come like a blight
Over thy spirit, and sad images
Of the stern agony, and shroud, and pall,
And breathless darkness, and the narrow house,
Make thee to shudder, and grow sick at heart ;—

Go forth, under the open sky, and list
To Nature's teachings, while from all around—
Earth and her waters, and the depths of air,—
Comes a still voice—Yet a few days, and thee
The all-beholding sun shall see no more
In all his course ; nor yet in the cold ground,
Where thy pale form was laid, with many tears,
Nor in the embrace of ocean, shall exist
Thy image.   Earth, that nourished thee, shall
          claim
Thy growth, to be resolved to earth again,
And, lost each human trace, surrendering up
Thine individual being, shalt thou go
To mix for ever with the elements,
To be a brother to the insensible rock
And to the sluggish clod, which the rude swain
Turns with his share, and treads upon.   The
          oak
Shall send his roots abroad, and pierce thy
          mould.

Yet not to thine eternal resting-place
Shalt thou retire alone,—nor couldst thou wish
Couch more magnificent. Thou shalt lie down
With patriarchs of the infant world—with kings,
The powerful of the earth—the wise, the good,
Fair forms, and hoary seers of ages past,
All in one mighty sepulchre. The hills
Rock-ribbed and ancient as the sun ; the vales
Stretching in pensive quietness between ;
The venerable woods ; rivers that move
In majesty, and the complaining brooks
That make the meadows green ; and, poured
        round all,
Old ocean's gray and melancholy waste,—
Are but the solemn decorations all
Of the great tomb of man. The golden sun,
The planets, all the infinite host of heaven.
Are shining on the sad abodes of death,
Through the still lapse of ages. All that tread
The globe are but a handful to the tribes

That slumber in its bosom.—Take the wings
Of morning, traverse Barca's desert sands,
Or lose thyself in the continuous woods
Where rolls the Oregan, and hears no sound,
Save his own dashings—yet—the dead are
        there :
And millions in those solitudes, since first
The flight of years began, have laid them down
In their last sleep—the dead reign there alone.
So shalt thou rest, and what if thou withdraw
In silence from the living, and no friend
Take note of thy departure ?   All that breathe
Will share thy destiny.   The gay will laugh
When thou art gone, the solemn brood of care
Plod on, and each one as before will chase
His favourite phantom ; yet all these shall leave
Their mirth and their employments, and shall
        come,
And make their bed with thee.   As the long
        train

Of ages glide away, the sons of men,
The youth in life's green spring, and he who
goes
In the full strength of years, matron, and maid
And the sweet babe, and the gray-headed
man,—
Shall one by one be gathered to thy side,
By those, who in their turn shall follow them.

So live, that when thy summons comes to join
The innumerable caravan, which moves
To that mysterious realm, where each shall take
His chamber in the silent halls of death,
Thou go not, like the quarry-slave at night,
Scourged to his dungeon, but, sustained and
soothed
By an unfaltering trust, approach thy grave
Like one who wraps the drapery of his couch
About him, and lies down to pleasant dreams

THE YELLOW VIOLET.

When beechen buds begin to swell,
  And woods the blue-bird's warble know,
The yellow violet's modest bell
  Peeps from the last year's leaves below.

Ere russet fields their green resume,
  Sweet flower, I love, in forest bare,
To meet thee, when thy faint perfume
  Alone is in the virgin air.

Of all her train, the hands of Spring
  First plant thee in the watery mould,
And I have seen thee blossoming
  Beside the snow-bank's edges cold.

Thy parent sun, who bade thee view
  Pale skies, and chilling moisture sip,
Has bathed thee in his own bright hue,
  And streaked with jet thy glowing lip.

Yet slight thy form, and low thy seat,
  And earthward bent thy gentle eye,
Unapt the passing view to meet,
  When loftier flowers are flaunting nigh.

Oft, in the sunless April day,
  Thy early smile has stayed my walk ;
But midst the gorgeous blooms of May,
  I passed thee on thy humble stalk.

So they, who climb to wealth, forget
    The friends in darker fortunes tried ;
I copied them—but I regret
    That I should ape the ways of pride.

And when again the genial hour
    Awakes the painted tribes of light,
I'll not o'erlook the modest flower
    That made the woods of April bright.

INSCRIPTION FOR THE ENTRANCE
TO A WOOD.

STRANGER, if thou hast learned a truth which
  needs
No school of long experience, that the world
Is full of guilt and misery, and hast seen
Enough of all its sorrows, crimes, and cares,
To tire thee of it, enter this wild wood
And view the haunts of Nature. The calm
  shade
Shall bring a kindred calm, and the sweet breeze

That makes the green leaves dance, shall waft
    a balm
To thy sick heart.   Thou wilt find nothing here
Of all that pained thee in the haunts of men
And made thee loathe thy life.   The primal
    curse
Fell, it is true, upon the unsinning earth,
But not in vengeance.   God hath yoked to guilt
Her pale tormentor, misery.   Hence these
    shades
Are still the abodes of gladness ; the thick roof
Of green and stirring branches is alive
And musical with birds, that sing and sport
In wantonness of spirit ; while below
The squirrel, with raised paws and form erect,
Chirps merrily.   Throngs of insects in the shade
Try their thin wings and dance in the warm
    beam
That waked them into life.   Even the green
    trees

Partake the deep contentment ; as they bend
To the soft winds, the sun from the blue sky
Looks in and sheds a blessing on the scene.
Scarce less the cleft-born wild-flower seems to
      enjoy
Existence, than the winged plunderer
That sucks its sweets.   The mossy rocks them-
      selves,
And the old and ponderous trunks of prostrate
      trees
That lead from knoll to knoll a causey rude,
Or bridge the sunken brook, and their dark
      roots,
With all their earth upon them, twisting high,
Breathe fixed tranquillity.   The rivulet
Sends forth glad sounds, and tripping o'er its
      bed
Of pebbly sands, or leaping down the rocks,
Seems, with continuous laughter, to rejoice
In its own being.   Softly tread the marge,

Lest from her midway perch thou scare the wren
That dips her bill in water.   The cool wind,
That stirs the stream in play, shall come to
        thee,
Like one that loves thee nor will let thee pass
Ungreeted, and shall give its light embrace.

SONG.

Soon as the glazed and gleaming snow
 Reflects the day-dawn cold and clear,
The hunter of the west must go
 In depth of woods to seek the deer.

His rifle on his shoulder placed,
 His stores of death arranged with skill,
His moccasins and snow-shoes laced,—
 Why lingers he beside the hill?

Far, in the dim and doubtful light,
  Where woody slopes a valley leave,
He sees what none but lover might,
  The dwelling of his Genevieve.

And oft he turns his truant eye,
  And pauses oft, and lingers near ;
But when he marks the reddening sky,
  He bounds away to hunt the deer.

TO A WATERFOWL.

Whither, midst falling dew,
While glow the heavens with the last steps of
        day,
Far, through their rosy depths, dost thou pursue
    Thy solitary way ?

    Vainly the fowler's eye
Might mark thy distant flight to do thee wrong,
As, darkly seen against the crimson sky,
    Thy figure floats along.

Seek'st thou the plashy brink
Of weedy lake, or marge of river wide,
Or where the rocking billows rise and sink
    On the chafed ocean side?

    There is a Power whose care
Teaches thy way along that pathless coast,—
The desert and illimitable air,—
    Lone wandering, but not lost.

    All day thy wings have fanned,
At that far height, the cold thin atmosphere,
Yet stoop not, weary, to the welcome land,
    Though the dark night is near.

    And soon that toil shall end;
Soon shalt thou find a summer home and rest,
And scream among thy fellows; reeds shall
        bend,
    Soon, o'er thy sheltered nest.

Thou'rt gone, the abyss of heaven
Hath swallowed up thy form ; yet, on my heart
Deeply hath sunk the lesson thou hast given,
    And shall not soon depart.

He who, from zone to zone,
Guides through the boundless sky thy certain
        flight,
In the long way that I must tread alone,
    Will lead my steps aright.

GREEN RIVER.

When breezes are soft and skies are fair,
I steal an hour from study and care,
And hie me away to the woodland scene,
Where wanders the stream with waters of green,
As if the bright fringe of herbs on its brink
Had given their stain to the wave they drink ;
And they, whose meadows it murmurs through,
Have named the stream from its own fair hue.

Yet pure its waters—its shallows are bright
With colored pebbles and sparkles of light,

And clear the depths where its eddies play,
And dimples deepen and whirl away,
And the plane-tree's speckled arms o'ershoot
The swifter current that mines its root,
Through whose shifting leaves, as you walk the
  hill,
The quivering glimmer of sun and rill
With a sudden flash on the eye is thrown,
Like the ray that streams from the diamond-
  stone.
Oh, loveliest there the spring days come,
With blossoms, and birds, and wild bees' hum ;
The flowers of summer are fairest there,
And freshest the breath of the summer air ;
And sweetest the golden autumn day
In silence and sunshine glides away.

Yet, fair as thou art, thou shunnest to glide,
Beautiful stream ! by the village side ;

But windest away from haunts of men,
To quiet valley and shaded glen ;
And forest, and meadow, and slope of hill,
Around thee, are lonely, lovely, and still.
Lonely, save when, by thy rippling tides,
From thicket to thicket the angler glides ;
Or the simpler comes, with basket and book,
For herbs of power on thy banks to look ;
Or haply, some idle dreamer, like me,
To wander, and muse, and gaze on thee.
Still—save the chirp of birds that feed
On the river cherry and seedy reed,
And thy own wild music gushing out
With mellow murmur or fairy shout,
From dawn to the blush of another day,
Like traveller singing along his way.

That fairy music I never hear,
Nor gaze on those waters so green and clear.

And mark them winding away from sight,
Darkened with shade or flashing with light,
While o'er them the vine to its thicket clings,
And the zephyr stoops to freshen his wings,
But I wish that fate had left me free
To wander these quiet haunts with thee,
Till the eating cares of earth should depart,
And the peace of the scene pass into my heart;
And I envy thy stream as it glides along,
Through its beautiful banks, in a trance of song.

  Though forced to drudge for the dregs of men,
And scrawl strange words with the barbarous pen,
And mingle among the jostling crowd,
Where the sons of strife are subtle and loud—
I often come to this quiet place,
To breathe the airs that ruffle thy face,
And gaze upon thee in silent dream,
For in thy lonely and lovely stream
An image of that calm life appears
That won my heart in my greener years.

A WINTER PIECE.

THE time has been that these wild solitudes,
Yet beautiful as wild, were trod by me
Oftener than now ; and when the ills of life
Had chafed my spirit—when the unsteady pulse
Beat with strange flutterings—1 would wander
        forth
And seek the woods.   The sunshine on my path
Was to me as a friend.   The swelling hills,
The quiet dells retiring far between,
With gentle invitation to explore

Their windings, were a calm society
That talked with me and soothed me. Then
the chant
Of birds, and chime of brooks, and soft caress
Of the fresh sylvan air, made me forget
The thoughts that broke my peace, and I began
To gather simples by the fountain's brink,
And lose myself in day-dreams. While I stood
In nature's loneliness, I was with one
With whom I early grew familiar, one
Who never had a frown for me, whose voice
Never rebuked me for the hours I stole
From cares I loved not, but of which the world
Deems highest, to converse with her. When
shrieked
The bleak November winds, and smote the
woods,
And the brown fields were herbless, and the
shades,
That met above the merry rivulet,

Were spoiled, I sought, I loved them still;
    they seemed
Like old companions in adversity.
Still there was beauty in my walks; the brook,
Bordered with sparkling frost-work, was as gay
As with its fringe of summer flowers. Afar,
The village with its spires, the path of streams,
And dim receding valleys, hid before
By interposing trees, lay visible
Through the bare grove, and my familiar haunts
Seemed new to me. Nor was I slow to come
Among them, when the clouds, from their still
    skirts,
Had shaken down on earth the feathery snow,
And all was white. The pure keen air abroad,
Albeit it breathed no scent of herb, nor heard
Love-call of bird nor merry hum of bee,
Was not the air of death. Bright mosses crept
Over the spotted trunks, and the close buds,
That lay along the boughs, instinct with life,

Patient, and waiting the soft breath of Spring,
Feared not the piercing spirit of the North.
The snow-bird twittered on the beechen bough,
And 'neath the hemlock, whose thick branches
        bent
Beneath its bright cold burden, and kept dry
A circle, on the earth, of withered leaves,
The partridge found a shelter. Through the
        snow
The rabbit sprang away. The lighter track
Of fox, and the racoon's broad path were there,
Crossing each other. From his hollow tree,
The squirrel was abroad, gathering the nuts
Just fallen, that asked the winter cold and sway
Of winter blast, to shake them from their hold.

But winter has yet brighter scenes,—he
        boasts
Splendors beyond what gorgeous Summer knows;
Or Autumn with his many fruits, and woods

All flushed with many hues.   Come when the
    rains
Have glazed the snow, and clothed the trees
    with ice ;
While the slant sun of February pours
Into the bowers a flood of light.   Approach !
The incrusted surface shall upbear thy steps,
And the broad arching portals of the grove
Welcome thy entering. Look ! the massy trunks
Are cased in the pure crystal ; each light spray,
Nodding and tinkling in the breath of heaven,
Is studded with its trembling water-drops,
That glimmer with an amethystine light.
But round the parent stem the long low boughs
Bend, in a glittering ring, and arbors hide
The glassy floor.   Oh ! you might deem the spot
The spacious cavern of some virgin mine,
Deep in the womb of earth—where the gems
    grow,
And diamonds put forth radiant rods and bud

With amethyst and topaz—and the place
Lit up, most royally, with the pure beam
That dwells in them. Or haply the vast hall
Of fairy palace, that outlasts the night,
And fades not in the glory of the sun ;—
Where crystal columns send forth slender shafts
And crossing arches ; and fantastic aisles
Wind from the sight in brightness, and are
        lost
Among the crowded pillars. Raise thine eye ;
Thou seest no cavern roof, no palace vault ;
There the blue sky and the white drifting cloud
Look in. Again the wildered fancy dreams
Of spouting fountains, frozen as they rose,
And fixed, with all their branching jets, in air,
And all their sluices sealed. All, all is light ;
Light without shade. But all shall pass away
With the next sun. From numberless vast
        trunks,
Loosened, the crashing ice shall make a sound

Like the far roar of rivers, and the eve
Shall close o'er the brown woods as it was wont.

And it is pleasant, when the noisy streams
Are just set free, and milder suns melt off
The plashy snow, save only the firm drift
In the deep glen or the close shade of pines,—
'Tis pleasant to behold the wreaths of smoke
Roll up among the maples of the hill,
Where the shrill sound of youthful voices wakes
The shriller echo, as the clear pure lymph,
That from the wounded trees, in twinkling
      drops,
Falls, mid the golden brightness of the morn,
Is gathered in with brimming pails, and oft,
Wielded by sturdy hands, the stroke of axe
Makes the woods ring. Along the quiet air,
Come and float calmly off the soft light clouds,
Such as you see in summer, and the winds
Scarce stir the branches. Lodged in sunny cleft,

Where the cold breezes come not, blooms alone
The little wind-flower, whose just opened eye
Is blue as the spring heaven it gazes at—
Startling the loiterer in the naked groves
With unexpected beauty, for the time
Of blossoms and green leaves is yet afar.
And ere it comes, the encountering winds shall
        oft
Muster their wrath again, and rapid clouds
Shade heaven, and bounding on the frozen earth
Shall fall their volleyed stores, rounded like hail
And white like snow, and the loud North again
Shall buffet the vexed forest in his rage.

THE WEST WIND.

BENEATH the forest's skirt I rest,
   Whose branching pines rise dark and high,
And hear the breezes of the West
   Among the thread-like foliage sigh.

Sweet Zephyr! why that sound of woe?
   Is not thy home among the flowers?
Do not the bright June roses blow,
   To meet thy kiss at morning hours?

And lo ! thy glorious realm outspread—
   Yon stretching valleys, green and gay,
And yon free hill-tops, o'er whose head
   The loose white clouds are borne away.

And there the full broad river runs,
   And many a fount wells fresh and sweet
To cool thee when the mid-day suns
   Have made thee faint beneath their heat.

Thou wind of joy, and youth, and love ;
   Spirit of the new-wakened year !
The sun, in his blue realm above,
   Smooths a bright path when thou art here.

In lawns the murmuring bee is heard,
   The wooing ring-dove in the shade ;
On thy soft breath the new-fledged bird
   Takes wing, half happy, half afraid.

Ah ! thou art like our wayward race ;—
　　When not a shade of pain or ill
Dims the bright smile of Nature's face,
　　Thou lov'st to sigh and murmur still.

THE BURIAL-PLACE.

A FRAGMENT.

Erewhile, on England's pleasant shores, our
    sires
Left not their churchyards unadorned with
    shades
Or blossoms ; and indulgent to the strong
And natural dread of man's last home, the grave,
Its frost and silence—they disposed around,
To soothe the melancholy spirit that dwelt
Too sadly on life's close, the forms and hues

Of vegetable beauty.   There the yew,
Green even amid the snows of winter, told
Of immortality, and gracefully
The willow, a perpetual mourner, drooped ;
And there the gadding woodbine crept about,
And there the ancient ivy.   From the spot
Where the sweet maiden, in her blossoming
      years
Cut off, was laid with streaming eyes, and hands
That trembled as they placed her there, the rose
Sprung modest, on bowed stalk, and better
      spoke
Her graces, than the proudest monument.
There children set about their playmate's grave
The pansy.   On the infant's little bed,
Wet at its planting with maternal tears,
Emblem of early sweetness, early death,
Nestled the lowly primrose.   Childless dames,
And maids that would not raise the reddened
      eye—

Orphans, from whose young lids the light of joy
Fled early,—silent lovers, who had given
All that they lived for to the arms of earth,
Came often, o'er the recent graves to strew
Their offerings, rue, and rosemary, and flowers.

The pilgrim bands who passed the sea to keep
Their Sabbaths in the eye of God alone,
In his wide temple of the wilderness,
Brought not these simple customs of the heart
With them. It might be, while they laid their
        dead
By the vast solemn skirts of the old groves,
And the fresh virgin soil poured forth strange
        flowers
About their graves ; and the familiar shades
Of their own native isle and wonted blooms
And herbs were wanting, which the pious hand
Might plant or scatter there, these gentle rites

Passed out of use.   Now they are scarcely
    known,
And rarely in our borders may you meet
The tall larch, sighing in the burying-place,
Or willow, trailing low its boughs to hide
The gleaming marble.   Naked rows of graves
And melancholy ranks of monuments
Are seen instead, where the coarse grass, be-
    tween,
Shoots up its dull green spikes, and in the wind
Hisses, and the neglected bramble nigh,
Offers its berries to the schoolboy's hand,
In vain—they grow too near the dead.   Yet here,
Nature, rebuking the neglect of man,
Plants often, by the ancient mossy stone,
The brier rose, and upon the broken turf
That clothes the fresher grave, the strawberry
    plant
Sprinkles its swell with blossoms, and lays forth
Her ruddy, pouting fruit.   *   *   *   *   *

"BLESSED ARE THEY THAT MOURN."

Oh, deem not they are blest alone
　　Whose lives a peaceful tenor keep ;
The Power who pities man, has shown
　　A blessing for the eyes that weep.

The light of smiles shall fill again
　　The lids that overflow with tears ;
And weary hours of woe and pain
　　Are promises of happier years.

There is a day of sunny rest
 For every dark and troubled night ;
And grief may bide an evening guest,
 But joy shall come with early light.

And thou, who, o'er thy friend's low bier,
 Sheddest the bitter drops like rain,
Hope that a brighter, happier sphere
 Will give him to thy arms again.

Nor let the good man's trust depart,
 Though life its common gifts deny,—
Though, with a pierced and bleeding heart,
 And spurned of men, he goes to die.

For God hath marked each sorrowing day
 And numbered every secret tear,
And heaven's long age of bliss shall pay
 For all his children suffer here.

"NO MAN KNOWETH HIS SEPUL-
CHRE."

WHEN he, who, from the scourge of wrong,
   Aroused the Hebrew tribes to fly,
Saw the fair region, promised long,
   And bowed him on the hills to die ;

God made his grave, to men unknown,
   Where Moab's rocks a vale infold,
And laid the aged seer alone
   To slumber while the world grows old.

Thus still, whene'er the good and just
  Close the dim eye on life and pain,
Heaven watches o'er their sleeping dust
  Till the pure spirit comes again.

Though nameless, trampled, and forgot,
  His servant's humble ashes lie,
Yet God has marked and sealed the spot,
  To call its inmate to the sky.

A WALK AT SUNSET.

When insect wings are glistening in the beam
    Of the low sun, and mountain-tops are bright,
Oh, let me, by the crystal valley-stream,
    Wander amid the mild and mellow light ;
And, while the wood-thrush pipes his evening lay,
Give me one lonely hour to hymn the setting day.

Oh, sun ! that o'er the western mountains now
    Go'st down in glory ! ever beautiful
And blessed is thy radiance, whether thou
    Colorest the eastern heaven and night-mist
        cool,

Till the bright day-star vanish, or on high
Climbest and streamest thy white splendors
      from mid sky.

Yet, loveliest are thy setting smiles, and fair,
    Fairest of all that earth beholds, the hues
That live among the clouds and flush the air,
    Lingering and deepening at the hour of dews.
Then softest gales are breathed, and softest
      heard
The plaining voice of streams and pensive note
      of bird.

They who here roamed, of yore, the forest wide,
    Felt, by such charm, their simple bosoms won ;
They deemed their quivered warrior, when he
      died,
    Went to bright isles beneath the setting
      sun ;

Where winds are aye at peace, and skies are fair,
And purple-skirted clouds curtain the crimson
    air.

So, with the glories of the dying day,
  Its thousand trembling lights and changing
    hues,
The memory of the brave who passed away
  Tenderly mingled ;—fitting hour to muse
On such grave theme, and sweet the dream
    that shed
Brightness and beauty round the destiny of the
    dead.

For ages, on the silent forests here,
  Thy beams did fall before the red man came
To dwell beneath them ; in their shade the
    deer
  Fed, and feared not the arrow's deadly aim.

Nor tree was felled in all that world of woods,
Save by the beaver's tooth, or winds, or rush of
    floods.

Then came the hunter tribes, and thou didst
    look,
  For ages, on their deeds in the hard chase,
And well-fought wars ; green sod and silver
    brook
  Took the first stain of blood ; before thy face
The warrior generations came and passed,
And glory was laid up for many an age to last.

Now they are gone, gone as thy setting blaze
  Goes down the west, while night is press-
    ing on,
And with them the old tale of better days
  And trophies of remembered power, are gone.

Yon field that gives the harvest, where the
    plough
Strikes the white bone, is all that tells their
    story now.

I stand upon their ashes in thy beam,
  The offspring of another race, I stand,
Beside a stream they loved, this valley stream ;
  And where the night-fires of the quivered
    band
Showed the gray oak by fits, and war-song
    rung,
I teach the quiet shades the strains of this new
    tongue.

Farewell ! but thou shalt come again ! thy
    light
  Must shine on other changes, and behold

The place of the thronged city still as night—
  States fallen—new empires built upon the
        old—
But never shalt thou see these realms again
Darkened by boundless groves, and roamed by
    savage men.

HYMN TO DEATH.

OH ! could I hope the wise and pure in heart
Might hear my song without a frown, nor deem
My voice unworthy of the theme it tries,—
I would take up the hymn to Death, and say
To the grim power, The world hath slandered
    thee
And mocked thee.   On thy dim and shadowy
    brow
They place an iron crown, and call thee king
Of terrors, and the spoiler of the world,
Deadly assassin, that strik'st down the fair,
The loved, the good—that breathest on the
    lights

Of virtue set along the vale of life,
And they go out in darkness.   I am come,
Not with reproaches, not with cries and prayers,
Such as have stormed thy stern, insensible ear
From the beginning ; I am come to speak
Thy praises.   True it is that I have wept
Thy conquests, and may weep them yet again ;
And thou from some I love wilt take a life
Dear to me as my own.   Yet while the spell
Is on my spirit, and I talk with thee
In sight of all thy trophies, face to face,
Meet is it that my voice should utter forth
Thy nobler triumphs ; I will teach the world
To thank thee.   Who are thine accusers ?—
     Who ?
The living !—they who never felt thy power,
And know thee not.   The curses of the wretch
Whose crimes are ripe, his sufferings when thy
     hand
Is on him, and the hour he dreads is come,

Are writ among thy praises.   But the good—
Does he whom thy kind hand dismissed to
      peace,
Upbraid the gentle violence that took off
His fetters, and unbarred his prison cell ?

      Raise then the hymn to Death.   Deliverer !
God hath anointed thee to free the oppressed
And crush the oppressor.   When the armed
      chief,
The conqueror of nations, walks the world,
And it is changed beneath his feet, and all
Its kingdoms melt into one mighty realm—
Thou, while his head is loftiest and his heart
Blasphemes, imagining his own right hand
Almighty, thou dost set thy sudden grasp
Upon him, and the links of that strong chain
Which bound mankind are crumbled ; thou
      dost break
      Vol. I.—4

Sceptre and crown, and beat his throne to dust.
Then the earth shouts with gladness, and her
      tribes
Gather within their ancient bounds again.
Else had the mighty of the olden time,
Nimrod, Sesostris, or the youth who feigned
His birth from Libyan Ammon, smitten yet
The nations with a rod of iron, and driven
The chariot o'er our necks.   Thou dost avenge,
In thy good time, the wrongs of those who know
No other friend.   Nor dost thou interpose
Only to lay the sufferer asleep,
Where he who made him wretched troubles not
His rest—thou dost strike down his tyrant too.
Oh, there is joy when hands that held the
      scourge
Drop lifeless, and the pitiless heart is cold.
Thou too dost purge from earth its horrible
And old idolatries ;—from the proud fanes
Each to his grave their priests go out, till none

Is left to teach their worship ; then the fires
Of sacrifice are chilled, and the green moss
O'ercreeps their altars ; the fallen images
Cumber the weedy courts, and for loud hymns,
Chanted by kneeling multitudes, the wind
Shrieks in the solitary aisles.   When he
Who gives his life to guilt, and laughs at all
The laws that God or man has made, and round
Hedges his seat with power, and shines in
      wealth,—
Lifts up his atheist front to scoff at Heaven,
And celebrates his shame in open day,
Thou, in the pride of all his crimes, cutt'st off
The horrible example.   Touched by thine
The extortioner's hard hand foregoes the gold
Wrung from the o'er-worn poor.   The perjurer
Whose tongue was lithe, even now, and voluble
Against his neighbor's life, and he who laughed
And leaped for joy to see a spotless fame
Blasted before his own foul calumnies,

Are smit with deadly silence. He, who sold
His conscience to preserve a worthless life,
Even while he hugs himself on his escape,
Trembles, as, doubly terrible, at length,
Thy steps o'ertake him, and there is no time
For parley—nor will bribes unclench thy grasp
Oft, too, dost thou reform thy victim, long
Ere his last hour. And when the reveller,
Mad in the chase of pleasure, stretches on,
And strains each nerve, and clears the path of
  life
Like wind, thou point'st him to the dreadful
  goal,
And shak'st thy hour-glass in his reeling eye,
And check'st him in mid course. Thy skeleton
  hand
Shows to the faint of spirit the right path,
And he is warned, and fears to step aside.
Thou sett'st between the ruffian and his crime
Thy ghastly countenance, and his slack hand

Drops the drawn knife. But, oh, most fear-
   fully
Dost thou show forth Heaven's justice, when
   thy shafts
Drink up the ebbing spirit—then the hard
Of heart and violent of hand restores
The treasure to the friendless wretch he wronged.
Then from the writhing bosom thou dost pluck
The guilty secret ; lips, for ages sealed,
Are faithless to the dreadful trust at length,
And give it up ; the felon's latest breath
Absolves the innocent man who bears his crime ;
The slanderer, horror-smitten, and in tears,
Recalls the deadly obloquy he forged
To work his brother's ruin. Thou dost make
Thy penitent victim utter to the air
The dark conspiracy that strikes at life,
And aims to whelm the laws ; ere yet the
   hour
Is come, and the dread sign of murder given.

Thus, from the first of time, hast thou been
        found
On virtue's side ; the wicked, but for thee,
Had been too strong for the good ; the great of
        earth
Had crushed the weak for ever.   Schooled in
        guile
For ages, while each passing year had brought
Its baneful lesson, they had filled the world
With their abominations ; while its tribes,
Trodden to earth, imbruted, and despoiled,
Had knelt to them in worship ; sacrifice
Had smoked on many an altar, temple roofs
Had echoed with the blasphemous prayer and
        hymn :
But thou, the great reformer of the world,
Tak'st off the sons of violence and fraud
In their green pupilage, their lore half learned—
Ere guilt had quite o'errun the simple heart
God gave them at their birth, and blotted out

His image. Thou dost mark them flushed with
    hope,
As on the threshold of their vast designs
Doubtful and loose they stand, and strik'st
    them down.

    ※   ※   ※   ※   ※

    Alas ! I little thought that the stern power
Whose fearful praise I sung, would try me thus
Before the strain was ended. It must cease—
For he is in his grave who taught my youth
The art of verse, and in the bud of life
Offered me to the muses. Oh, cut off
Untimely ! when thy reason in its strength,
Ripened by years of toil and studious search
And watch of Nature's silent lessons, taught
Thy hand to practise best the lenient art
To which thou gavest thy laborious days,
And, last, thy life. And, therefore, when the
    earth

Received thee, tears were in unyielding eyes
And on hard cheeks, and they who deemed thy
  skill
Delayed their death-hour, shuddered and turned
  pale
When thou wert gone.   This faltering verse,
  which thou
Shalt not, as wont, o'erlook, is all I have
To offer at thy grave—this—and the hope
To copy thy example, and to leave
A name of which the wretched shall not think
As of an enemy's, whom they forgive
As all forgive the dead.   Rest, therefore, thou
Whose early guidance trained my infant steps—
Rest, in the bosom of God, till the brief sleep
Of death is over, and a happier life
Shall dawn to waken thine insensible dust.

 Now thou art not—and yet the men whose
  guilt

Has wearied Heaven for vengeance—he who
      bears
False witness—he who takes the orphan's bread,
And robs the widow—he who spreads abroad
Polluted hands in mockery of prayer,
Are left to cumber earth.   Shuddering I look
On what is written, yet I blot not out
The desultory numbers ; let them stand,
The record of an idle revery.

THE MASSACRE AT SCIO.

WEEP not for Scio's children slain ;
　　Their blood, by Turkish falchions shed,
Sends not its cry to Heaven in vain
　　For vengeance on the murderer's head.

Though high the warm red torrent ran
　　Between the flames that lit the sky,
Yet, for each drop, an armed man
　　Shall rise, to free the land, or die.

And for each corpse, that in the sea
  Was thrown, to feast the scaly herds,
A hundred of the foe shall be
  A banquet for the mountain birds.

Stern rites and sad shall Greece ordain
  To keep that day, along her shore,
Till the last link of slavery's chain
  Is shivered, to be worn no more.

THE INDIAN GIRL'S LAMENT.

An Indian girl was sitting where
    Her lover, slain in battle, slept ;
Her maiden veil, her own black hair,
    Came down o'er eyes that wept ;
And wildly, in her woodland tongue,
This sad and simple lay she sung :

" I've pulled away the shrubs that grew
    Too close above thy sleeping head,
And broke the forest boughs that threw
    Their shadows o'er thy bed,
That, shining from the sweet south-west,
The sunbeams might rejoice thy rest.

" It was a weary, weary road
    That led thee to the pleasant coast,
  Where thou, in his serene abode,
    Hast met thy father's ghost ;
  Where everlasting autumn lies
  On yellow woods and sunny skies.

" 'Twas I the broidered mocsen made,
    That shod thee for that distant land ;
  'Twas I thy bow and arrows laid
    Beside thy still cold hand ;
  Thy bow in many a battle bent,
  Thy arrows never vainly sent.

" With wampum belts I crossed thy breast,
    And wrapped thee in the bison's hide,
  And laid the food that pleased thee best,
    In plenty, by thy side,
  And decked thee bravely, as became
  A warrior of illustrious name.

" Thou'rt happy now, for thou hast passed
    The long dark journey of the grave,
And in the land of light, at last,
    Hast joined the good and brave ;
Amid the flushed and balmy air,
The bravest and the loveliest there.

" Yet, oft to thine own Indian maid
    Even there thy thoughts will earthward
        stray,—
To her who sits where thou wert laid,
    And weeps the hours away,
Yet almost can her grief forget,
To think that thou dost love her yet.

" And thou, by one of those still lakes
    That in a shining cluster lie,
On which the south wind scarcely breaks
    The image of the sky,
A bower for thee and me hast made
Beneath the many-colored shade.

" And thou dost wait and watch to meet
  My spirit sent to join the blest,
And, wondering what detains my feet
  From the bright land of rest,
Dost seem, in every sound, to hear
The rustling of my footsteps near "

ODE FOR AN AGRICULTURAL CELE-
BRATION.

Far back in the ages,
   The plough with wreaths was crowned ;
The hands of kings and sages
   Entwined the chaplet round ;
Till men of spoil disdained the toil
   By which the world was nourished,
And dews of blood enriched the soil
   Where green their laurels flourished.
—Now the world her fault repairs—
   The guilt that stains her story,
And weeps her crimes amid the cares
   That formed her earliest glory.

The proud throne shall crumble,
  The diadem shall wane,
The tribes of earth shall humble
  The pride of those who reign ;
And War shall lay his pomp away ;—
  The fame that heroes cherish,
The glory earned in deadly fray
  Shall fade, decay, and perish.
Honor waits, o'er all the Earth,
  Through endless generations,
The art that calls her harvests forth,
  And feeds the expectant nations.

RIZPAH.

And he delivered them into the hands of the Gibeonites, and they hang-
ed them on the hill before the Lord ; and they fell all seven together, and
were put to death in the days of the harvest, in the first days, in the begin-
ning of barley-harvest.

And Rizpah, the daughter of Aiah, took sackcloth, and spread it for her
upon the rock, from the beginning of harvest until the water dropped up-
on them out of heaven, and suffered neither the birds of the air to rest
upon them by day, nor the beasts of the field by night.

2 Samuel, xxi. 10.

Hear what the desolate Rizpah said,

As on Gibeah's rocks she watched the dead.

The sons of Michal before her lay,

And her own fair children, dearer than they ;

By a death of shame they all had died,
And were stretched on the bare rock, side by
    side;
And Rizpah, once the loveliest of all
That bloomed and smiled in the court of Saul.
All wasted with watching and famine now,
And scorched by the sun her haggard brow,
Sat mournfully guarding their corpses there,
And murmured a strange and solemn air;
The low, heart-broken and wailing strain
Of a mother that mourns her children slain:

"I have made the crags my home and spread
On their desert backs my sackloth bed;
I have eaten the bitter herb of the rocks,
And drunk the midnight dew in my locks;
I have wept till I could not weep, and the pain
Of my burning eyeballs went to my brain.
Seven blackened corpses before me lie,
In the blaze of the sun and the winds of the sky.

I have watched them through the burning
      day,
And driven the vulture and raven away ;
And the cormorant wheeled in circles round,
Yet feared to light on the guarded ground.
And when the shadows of twilight came,
I have seen the hyena's eyes of flame,
And heard at my side his stealthy tread,
But aye at my shout the savage fled :
And I threw the lighted brand to fright
The jackal and wolf that yelled in the night.

" Ye were foully murdered, my hapless sons,
By the hands of wicked and cruel ones ;
Ye fell, in your fresh and blooming prime,
All innocent, for your father's crime.
He sinned—but he paid the price of his guilt
When his blood by a nameless hand was spilt ;
When he strove with the heathen host in vain,
And fell with the flower of his people slain,

And the sceptre his children's hands should
        sway
From his injured lineage passed away.

" But I hoped that the cottage roof would be
A safe retreat for my sons and me ;
And that while they ripened to manhood fast,
They should wean my thoughts from the woes
        of the past.
And my bosom swelled with a mother's pride,
As they stood in their beauty and strength by
        my side,
Tall like their sire, with the princely grace
Of his stately form, and the bloom of his face.

" Oh, what an hour for a mother's heart,
When the pitiless ruffians tore us apart !
When I clasped their knees and wept and
        prayed,
And struggled and shrieked to Heaven for aid,

And clung to my sons with desperate strength,
Till the murderers loosed my hold at length,
And bore me breathless and faint aside,
In their iron arms, while my children died.
They died—and the mother that gave them birth
Is forbidden to cover their bones with earth.

" The barley harvest was nodding white,
When my children died on the rocky height,
And the reapers were singing on hill and plain,
When I came to my task of sorrow and pain.
But now the season of rain is nigh,
The sun is dim in the thickening sky,
And the clouds in sullen darkness rest
Where he hides his light at the doors of the west
I hear the howl of the wind that brings
The long drear storm on its heavy wings ;
But the howling wind and the driving rain
Will beat my houseless head in vain ;
I shall stay, from my murdered sons to scare
The beasts of the desert, and fowls of air."

THE OLD MAN'S FUNERAL.

I saw an aged man upon his bier,
  His hair was thin and white, and on his brow
A record of the cares of many a year ;—
  Cares that were ended and forgotten now.
And there was sadness round, and faces bowed,
And woman's tears fell fast, and children wailed
    aloud.

Then rose another hoary man and said,
  In faltering accents, to that weeping train,

" Why mourn ye that our aged friend is dead ?
    Ye are not sad to see the gathered grain,
Nor when their mellow fruit the orchards cast,
Nor when the yellow woods shake down the
        ripened mast.

" Ye sigh not when the sun, his course fulfilled,
    His glorious course, rejoicing earth and sky,
In the soft evening, when the winds are stilled,
    Sinks where his islands of refreshment lie,
And leaves the smile of his departure spread
O'er the warm-colored heaven and ruddy moun-
        tain head.

" Why weep ye then for him, who, having won
    The bound of man's appointed years, at last,
Life's blessings all enjoyed, life's labors done,
    Serenely to his final rest has passed ;
While the soft memory of his virtues, yet,
Lingers like twilight hues, when the bright sun
        is set ?

" His youth was innocent ; his riper age
　　Marked with some act of goodness every day ;
And watched by eyes that loved him, calm and
　　　　sage,
　　Faded his last declining years away.
Cheerful he gave his being up, and went
To share the holy rest that waits a life well
　　　spent.

"That life was happy ; every day he gave
　　Thanks for the fair existence that was his ;
For a sick fancy made him not her slave,
　　To mock him with her phantom miseries.
No chronic tortures racked his aged limb,
For luxury and sloth had nourished none for
　　him.

" And I am glad that he has lived thus long,
　　And glad that he has gone to his reward ;
　　　Vol. I.—5

Nor can I deem that nature did him wrong,
  Softly to disengage the vital cord.
For when his hand grew palsied, and his eye
Dark with the mists of age, it was his time to
    die."

THE RIVULET.

This little rill, that from the springs
Of yonder grove its current brings,
Plays on the slope a while, and then
Goes prattling into groves again,
Oft to its warbling waters drew
My little feet, when life was new.
When woods in early green were dressed,
And from the chambers of the west
The warmer breezes, travelling out,
Breathed the new scent of flowers about,

My truant steps from home would stray,
Upon its grassy side to play,
List the brown thrasher's vernal hymn,
And crop the violet on its brim,
With blooming cheek and open brow,
As young and gay, sweet rill as thou.

    And when the days of boyhood came,
And I had grown in love with fame,
Duly I sought thy banks, and tried
My first rude numbers by thy side.
Words cannot tell how bright and gay
The scenes of life before me lay.
Then glorious hopes, that now to speak
Would bring the blood into my cheek,
Passed o'er me ; and I wrote, on high,
A name I deemed should never die.

    Years change thee not.   Upon yon hill
The tall old maples, verdant still,

Yet tell, in grandeur of decay,
How swift the years have passed away,
Since first, a child, and half afraid,
I wandered in the forest shade.
Thou, ever joyous rivulet,
Dost dimple, leap, and prattle yet;
And sporting with the sands that pave
The windings of thy silver wave,
And dancing to thy own wild chime,
Thou laughest at the lapse of time.
The same sweet sounds are in my ear
My early childhood loved to hear;
As pure thy limpid waters run;
As bright they sparkle to the sun;
As fresh and thick the bending ranks
Of herbs that line thy oozy banks;
The violet there, in soft May dew,
Comes up, as modest and as blue;
As green amid thy current's stress,
Floats the scarce-rooted watercress;

And the brown ground-bird, in thy glen,
Still chirps as merrily as then.

   Thou changest not—but I am changed,
Since first thy pleasant banks I ranged :
And the grave stranger, come to see
The play-place of his infancy,
Has scarce a single trace of him
Who sported once upon thy brim.
The visions of my youth are past—
Too bright, too beautiful to last.
I've tried the world—it wears no more
The coloring of romance it wore.
Yet well has Nature kept the truth
She promised to my earliest youth.
The radiant beauty shed abroad
On all the glorious works of God,
Shows freshly, to my sobered eye,
Each charm it wore in days gone by.

A few brief years shall pass away,
And I, all trembling, weak, and gray,
Bowed to the earth, which waits to fold
My ashes in the embracing mould,
(If haply the dark will of fate
Indulge my life so long a date,)
May come for the last time to look
Upon my childhood's favorite brook.
Then dimly on my eye shall gleam
The sparkle of thy dancing stream ;
And faintly on my ear shall fall
Thy prattling current's merry call ;
Yet shalt thou flow as glad and bright
As when thou met'st my infant sight.

And I shall sleep—and on thy side,
As ages after ages glide,
Children their early sports shall try,
And pass to hoary age and die.

But thou, unchanged from year to year,
Gayly shalt play and glitter here ;
Amid young flowers and tender grass
Thy endless infancy shalt pass ;
And, singing down thy narrow glen,
Shalt mock the fading race of men.

MARCH.

THE stormy March is come at last,
  With wind, and cloud, and changing skies,
I hear the rushing of the blast,
  That through the snowy valley flies.

Ah, passing few are they who speak,
  Wild stormy month ! in praise of thee ;
Yet, though thy winds are loud and bleak,
  Thou art a welcome month to me.

For thou, to northern lands, again
   The glad and glorious sun dost bring,
And thou hast joined the gentle train
   And wear'st the gentle name of Spring.

And, in thy reign of blast and storm,
   Smiles many a long, bright, sunny day,
When the changed winds are soft and warm,
   And heaven puts on the blue of May.

Then sing aloud the gushing rills,
   In joy that they again are free,
And brightly leaping down the hills,
   Begin their journey to the sea.

The year's departing beauty hides
   Of wintry storms the sullen threat ;
But in thy sternest frown abides
   A look of kindly promise yet.

Thou bring'st the hope of those calm skies
    And that soft time of sunny showers,
When the wide bloom, on earth that lies,
    Seems of a brighter world than ours.

CONSUMPTION.

Ay, thou art for the grave ; thy glances shine
  Too brightly to shine long ; another Spring
Shall deck her for men's eyes, but not for thine—
  Sealed in a sleep which knows no wakening.
The fields for thee have no medicinal leaf,
  And the vexed ore no mineral of power ;
And they who love thee wait in anxious grief
  Till the slow plague shall bring the fatal hour.
Glide softly to thy rest then; Death should come,
  Gently, to one of gentle mould like thee,

As light winds wandering through groves of
    bloom
  Detach the delicate blossom from the tree.
Close thy sweet eyes, calmly, and without pain ;
And we will trust in God to see thee yet again.

AN INDIAN STORY.

" I KNOW where the timid fawn abides
   In the depths of the shaded dell,
Where the leaves are broad and the thicket hides,
With its many stems and its tangled sides,
   From the eye of the hunter well.

" I know where the young May violet grows,
   In its lone and lowly nook,
On the mossy bank, where the larch-tree throws
Its broad dark boughs, in solemn repose,
   Far over the silent brook.

" And that timid fawn starts not with fear
    When I steal to her secret bower ;
And that young May violet to me is dear,
And I visit the silent streamlet near,
    To look on the lovely flower."

Thus Maquon sings as he lightly walks
    To the hunting ground on the hills ;
'Tis a song of his maid of the woods and rocks,
With her bright black eyes and long black locks,
    And voice like the music of rills.

He goes to the chase—but evil eyes
    Are at watch in the thicker shades ;
For she was lovely that smiled on his sighs,
And he bore, from a hundred lovers, his prize,
    The flower of the forest maids.

The boughs in the morning wind are stirred,
    And the woods their song renew,

With the early carol of many a bird,
And the quickened tune of the streamlet heard
  Where the hazels trickle with dew.

And Maquon has promised his dark-haired
      maid,
  Ere eve shall redden the sky,
A good red deer from the forest shade,
That bounds with the herd through grove and
      glade,
  At her cabin-door shall lie.

The hollow woods, in the setting sun,
  Ring shrill with the fire-bird's lay ;
And Maquon's sylvan labors are done,
And his shafts are spent, but the spoil they won
  He bears on his homeward way.

He stops near his bower—his eye perceives
  Strange traces along the ground—

At once to the earth his burden he heaves,
He breaks through the veil of boughs and
  leaves,
  And gains its door with a bound.

But the vines are torn on its walls that leant,
  And all from the young shrubs there
By struggling hands have the leaves been rent,
And there hangs on the sassafras, broken and
  bent,
  One tress of the well-known hair.

But where is she who, at this calm hour,
  Ever watched his coming to see ?
She is not at the door, nor yet in the bower ;
He calls—but he only hears on the flower
  The hum of the laden bee.

It is not a time for idle grief,
  Nor a time for tears to flow ;

The horror that freezes his limbs is brief—
He grasps his war-axe and bow, and a sheaf
   Of darts made sharp for the foe.

And he looks for the print of the ruffian's feet,
   Where he bore the maiden away ;
And he darts on the fatal path more fleet
Than the blast that hurries the vapor and sleet
   O'er the wild November day.

'Twas early summer when Maquon's bride
   Was stolen away from his door ;
But at length the maples in crimson are dyed,
And the grape is black on the cabin side,—
   And she smiles at his hearth once more.

But far in the pine-grove, dark and cold,
   Where the yellow leaf falls not,
Nor the autumn shines in scarlet and gold,
There lies a hillock of fresh dark mould,
   In the deepest gloom of the spot.

And the Indian girls, that pass that way,
    Point out the ravisher's grave ;
" And how soon to the bower she loved," they
        say,
" Returned the maid that was borne away
    From Maquon, the fond and the brave."

SUMMER WIND.

IT is a sultry day ; the sun has drunk
The dew that lay upon the morning grass ;
There is no rustling in the lofty elm
That canopies my dwelling, and its shade
Scarce cools me.   All is silent save the faint
And interrupted murmur of the bee,
Settling on the sick flowers, and then again
Instantly on the wing.   The plants around
Feel the too potent fervors ; the tall maize
Rolls up its long green leaves ; the clover droops

Its tender foliage, and declines its blooms.
But far, in the fierce sunshine, tower the hills,
With all their growth of woods, silent and stern ;
As if the scorching heat and dazzling light
Were but an element they loved. Bright clouds,
Motionless pillars of the brazen heaven,—
Their bases on the mountains—their white tops
Shining in the far ether—fire the air
With a reflected radiance, and make turn
The gazer's eyes away.   For me, I lie
Languidly in the shade, where the thick turf,
Yet virgin from the kisses of the sun,
Retains some freshness, and I woo the wind
That still delays his coming.   Why so slow,
Gentle and voluble spirit of the air ?
Oh, come and breathe upon the fainting earth
Coolness and life.   Is it that in his caves
He hears me ?   See, on yonder woody ridge,
The pine is bending his proud top, and now
Among the nearer groves, chestnut and oak

Are tossing their green boughs about. He comes!
Lo, where the grassy meadow runs in waves !
The deep distressful silence of the scene
Breaks up with mingling of unnumbered sounds
And universal motion.   He is come,
Shaking a shower of blossoms from the shrubs,
And bearing on their fragrance ; and he brings
Music of birds, and rustling of young boughs,
And sound of swaying branches, and the voice
Of distant waterfalls.   All the green herbs
Are stirring in his breath ; a thousand flowers,
By the road-side and the borders of the brook,
Nod gayly to each other ; glossy leaves
Are twinkling in the sun, as if the dew
Were on them yet, and silver waters break
Into small waves and sparkle as he comes.

AN INDIAN AT THE BURIAL PLACE
OF HIS FATHERS.

IT is the spot I came to seek,—
　My fathers' ancient burial place,
Ere from these vales, ashamed and weak,
　Withdrew our wasted race.
It is the spot—I know it well—
Of which our old traditions tell.

For here the upland bank sends out
　A ridge toward the river side ;
I know the shaggy hills about,

The meadows smooth and wide,
The plains, that, toward the southern sky,
Fenced east and west by mountains lie.

A white man gazing on the scene,
    Would say a lovely spot was here,
And praise the lawns so fresh and green,
    Between the hills so sheer.
I like it not—I would the plain
Lay in its tall old groves again.

The sheep are on the slopes around,
    The cattle in the meadows feed,
And laborers turn the crumbling ground,
    Or drop the yellow seed,
And prancing steeds, in trappings gay,
Whirl the bright chariot o'er the way.

Methinks it were a nobler sight
    To see these vales in woods arrayed,

Their summits in the golden light,
  Their trunks in grateful shade,
And herds of deer, that bounding go
O'er rocks and prostrate trees below.

And then to mark the lord of all,
  The forest hero, trained to wars,
Quivered and plumed, and lithe and tall,
  And seamed with glorious scars,
Walk forth, amid his reign, to dare
The wolf, and grapple with the bear.

This bank, in which the dead were laid,
  Was sacred when its soil was ours ;
Hither the silent Indian maid
  Brought wreaths of beads and flowers,
And the gay chief and gifted seer
Worshipped the God of thunders here.

But now the wheat is green and high,
  On clods that hid the warrior's breast,
And scattered in the furrows lie
  The weapons of his rest ;
And there, in the loose sand, is thrown
Of his large arm the mouldering bone.

Ah, little thought the strong and brave
  Who bore their lifeless chieftain forth,
Or the young wife, that weeping gave
  Her first-born to the earth,
That the pale race, who waste us now,
Among their bones should guide the plough

They waste us—ay—like April snow
  In the warm noon, we shrink away ;
And fast they follow, as we go
  Towards the setting day,—
Till they shall fill the land, and we
Are driven into the western sea.

But I behold a fearful sign,
　　To which the white men's eyes are blind ;
Their race may vanish hence, like mine,
　　And leave no trace behind,
Save ruins o'er the region spread,
And the white stones above the dead.

Before these fields were shorn and tilled,
　　Full to the brim our rivers flowed ;
The melody of waters filled
　　The fresh and boundless wood ;
And torrents dashed and rivulets played,
And fountains spouted in the shade.

Those grateful sounds are heard no more,
　　The springs are silent in the sun ;
The rivers, by the blackened shore,
　　With lessening current run ;
The realm our tribes are crushed to get
May be a barren desert yet.

SONG.

Dost thou idly ask to hear
   At what gentle seasons
Nymphs relent, when lovers near
   Press the tenderest reasons?
Ah, they give their faith too oft
   To the careless wooer;
Maidens' hearts are always soft:
   Would that men's were truer.

Woo the fair one, when around
   Early birds are singing;

When, o'er all the fragrant ground,
　Early herbs are springing ;
When the brookside, bank, and grove,
　All with blossoms laden,
Shine with beauty, breathe of love—
　Woo the timid maiden.

Woo her when, with rosy blush,
　Summer eve is sinking ;
When, on rills that softly gush,
　Stars are softly winking ;
When, through boughs that knit the bower,
　Moonlight gleams are stealing ;
Woo her, till the gentle hour
　Wake a gentler feeling.

Woo her, when autumnal dyes
　Tinge the woody mountain ;
When the dropping foliage lies
　In the weedy fountain ;

Let the scene, that tells how fast
　　Youth is passing over,
Warn her, ere her bloom is past,
　　To secure her lover.

Woo her, when the north winds call
　　At the lattice nightly ;
When, within the cheerful hall,
　　Blaze the fagots brightly ;
While the wintry tempest round
　　Sweeps the landscape hoary,
Sweeter in her ear shall sound
　　Love's delightful story.

HYMN OF THE WALDENSES.

Hear, Father, hear thy faint afflicted flock
Cry to thee, from the desert and the rock ;
While those, who seek to slay thy children, hold
Blasphemous worship under roofs of gold ;
And the broad goodly lands, with pleasant airs
That nurse the grape and wave the grain, are
        theirs.

Yet better were this mountain wilderness,
And this wild life of danger and distress—
Watchings by night and perilous flight by day,

And meetings in the depths of earth to pray,
Better, far better, than to kneel with them,
And pay the impious rite thy laws condemn.

Thou, Lord, dost hold the thunder ; the firm
          land
Tosses in billows when it feels thy hand ;
Thou dashest nation against nation, then
Stillest the angry world to peace again.
Or, touch their stony hearts who hunt thy sons—
The murderers of our wives and little ones.

Yet, mighty God, yet shall thy frown look forth
Unveiled, and terribly shall shake the earth.
Then the foul power of priestly sin and all
Its long-upheld idolatries shall fall.
Thou shalt raise up the trampled and oppressed,
And thy delivered saints shall dwell in rest.

MONUMENT MOUNTAIN.

THOU who wouldst see the lovely and the wild
Mingled in harmony on Nature's face,
Ascend our rocky mountains.   Let thy foot
Fail not with weariness, for on their tops
The beauty and the majesty of earth
Spread wide beneath, shall make thee to forget
The steep and toilsome way.   There, as thou
       stand'st,
The haunts of men below thee, and around
The mountain summits, thy expanding heart

Shall feel a kindred with that loftier world
To which thou art translated, and partake
The enlargement of thy vision. Thou shalt look
Upon the green and rolling forest tops,
And down into the secrets of the glens,
And streams, that with their bordering thickets strive
      strive
To hide their windings. Thou shalt gaze, at once,
      once,
Here on white villages, and tilth, and herds,
And swarming roads, and there on solitudes
That only hear the torrent, and the wind,
And eagle's shriek. There is a precipice
That seems a fragment of some mighty wall
Built by the hand that fashioned the old world,
To separate its nations, and thrown down
When the flood drowned them. To the north
      a path
Conducts you up the narrow battlement.
Steep is the western side, shaggy and wild

With mossy trees, and pinnacles of flint,
And many a hanging crag.   But, to the east,
Sheer to the vale go down the bare old cliffs,—
Huge pillars, that in middle heaven upbear
Their weather-beaten capitals, here dark
With moss, the growth of centuries, and there
Of chalky whiteness where the thunderbolt
Has splintered them.   It is a fearful thing
To stand upon the beetling verge, and see
Where storm and lightning, from that huge
          gray wall,
Have tumbled down vast blocks, and at the base
Dashed them in fragments, and to lay thine ear
Over the dizzy depth, and hear the sound
Of winds that struggle with the woods below,
Come up like ocean murmurs.   But the scene
Is lovely round ; a beautiful river there
Wanders amid the fresh and fertile meads,
The paradise he made unto himself,
Mining the soil for ages.   On each side

The fields swell upward to the hills ; beyond,
Above the hills, in the blue distance, rise
The mountain columns with which earth props
     heaven.

   There is a tale about these reverend rocks,
A sad tradition of unhappy love,
And sorrows borne and ended, long ago,
When over these fair vales the savage sought
His game in the thick woods. There was a maid,
The fairest of the Indian maids, bright-eyed,
With wealth of raven tresses, a light form,
And a gay heart. About her cabin door
The wide old woods resounded with her song
And fairy laughter all the summer day.
She loved her cousin ; such a love was deemed,
By the morality of those stern tribes,
Incestuous, and she struggled hard and long
Against her love, and reasoned with her heart,
As simple Indian maiden might. In vain.

Then her eye lost its lustre, and her step
Its lightness, and the gray-haired men that
      passed
Her dwelling, wondered that they heard no more
The accustomed song and laugh of her whose
      looks
Were like the cheerful smile of Spring, they
      said,
Upon the winter of their age. She went
To weep, where no eye saw, and was not found
When all the merry girls were met to dance,
And all the hunters of the tribe were out ;
Nor when they gathered from the rustling husk
The shining ear ; nor when, by the river's side,
They pulled the grape and startled the wild
      shades
With sounds of mirth. The keen-eyed Indian
      dames
Would whisper to each other, as they saw
Her wasting form, and say *the girl will die!*

One day into the bosom of a friend,
A playmate of her young and innocent years,
She poured her griefs. " Thou know'st, and
        thou alone,"
She said, " for I have told thee all, my love
And guilt and sorrow.   I am sick of life.
All night I weep in darkness, and the morn
Glares on me, as upon a thing accursed,
That has no business on the earth.   I hate
The pastimes and the pleasant toils that once
I loved ; the cheerful voices of my friends
Sound in my ear like mockings, and, at night,
In dreams, my mother, from the land of souls,
Calls me and chides me.   All that look on me
Do seem to know my shame ; I cannot bear
Their eyes ; I cannot from my heart root out
The love that wrings it so, and I must die."

It was a summer morning, and they went
To this old precipice.   About the cliffs

Lay garlands, ears of maize, and shaggy skins
Of wolf and bear, the offerings of the tribe
Here made to the Great Spirit, for they deemed,
Like worshippers of the elder time, that God
Doth walk on the high places and affect
The earth-o'erlooking mountains.   She had on
The ornaments with which her father loved
To deck the beauty of his bright-eyed girl,
And bade her wear when stranger warriors came
To be his guests.   Here the friends sat them
        down,
And sang, all day, old songs of love and death,
And decked the poor wan victim's hair with
        flowers,
And prayed that safe and swift might be her
        way
To that calm world of sunshine, where no grief
Makes the heart heavy and the eyelids red.
Beautiful lay the region of her tribe
Below her—waters resting in the embrace

Of the wide forest, and maize-planted glades
Opening amid the leafy wilderness.
She gazed upon it long, and at the sight
Of her own village peeping through the trees,
And her own dwelling, and the cabin roof
Of him she loved with an unlawful love,
And came to die for, a warm gush of tears
Ran from her eyes.   But when the sun grew low
And the hill shadows long, she threw herself
From the steep rock and perished.   There was
        scooped
Upon the mountain's southern slope, a grave ;
And there they laid her, in the very garb
With which the maiden decked herself for death,
With the same withering wild flowers in her hair.
And o'er the mould that covered her, the tribe
Built up a simple monument, a cone
Of small loose stones.   Thenceforward all who
        passed,
Hunter, and dame, and virgin, laid a stone

In silence on the pile. It stands there yet.
And Indians from the distant West, who come
To visit where their fathers' bones are laid,
Yet tell the sorrowful tale, and to this day
The mountain where the hapless maiden died
Is called the Mountain of the Monument.

AFTER A TEMPEST.

THE day had been a day of wind and storm ;
The wind was laid, the storm was overpast,
And stooping from the zenith, bright and warm,
Shone the great sun on the wide earth at last.
I stood upon the upland slope, and cast
My eye upon a broad and beauteous scene,
Where the vast plain lay girt by mountains vast,
And hills o'er hills lifted their heads of green,
With pleasant vales scooped out and villages
    between.

The rain-drops glistened on the trees around,
Whose shadows on the tall grass were not stirred,
Save when a shower of diamonds, to the ground,
Was shaken by the flight of startled bird ;
For birds were warbling round, and bees were
        heard
About the flowers ; the cheerful rivulet sung
And gossiped, as he hastened ocean-ward ;
To the gray oak the squirrel, chiding, clung,
And chirping from the ground the grasshopper
        upsprung.

And from beneath the leaves that kept them
        dry
Flew many a glittering insect here and there,
And darted up and down the butterfly,
That seemed a living blossom of the air.
The flocks came scattering from the thicket,
        where
The violent rain had pent them ; in the way

Strolled groups of damsels frolicsome and fair ;
The farmer swung the scythe or turned the hay ;
And 'twixt the heavy swaths the children were
    at play.

It was a scene of peace—and, like a spell,
Did that serene and golden sunlight fall
Upon the motionless wood that clothed the fell,
And precipice upspringing like a wall,
And glassy river and white waterfall,
And happy living things that trod the bright
And beauteous scene ; while far beyond them all,
On many a lovely valley, out of sight,
Was poured from the blue heavens the same
    soft golden light.

I looked, and thought the quiet of the scene
An emblem of the peace that yet shall be,
When o'er earth's continents, and isles between,
The noise of war shall cease from sea to sea,

And married nations dwell in harmony ;
When millions, crouching in the dust to one,
No more shall beg their lives on bended knee,
Nor the black stake be dressed, nor in the sun
The o'erlabored captive toil, and wish his life
      were done.

Too long, at clash of arms amid her bowers
And pools of blood, the earth has stood aghast,
The fair earth, that should only blush with
      flowers
And ruddy fruits ; but not for aye can last
The storm, and sweet the sunshine when 'tis
      past.
Lo, the clouds roll away—they break—they fly,
And, like the glorious light of summer, cast
O'er the wide landscape from the embracing sky,
On all the peaceful world the smile of heaven
      shall lie.

AUTUMN WOODS.

Ere, in the northern gale,
The summer tresses of the trees are gone,
The woods of Autumn, all around our vale,
Have put their glory on.

The mountains that infold,
In their wide sweep, the colored landscape round,
Seem groups of giant kings, in purple and gold,
That guard the enchanted ground.

I roam the woods that crown
The upland, where the mingled splendors glow,
Where the gay company of trees look down
    On the green fields below.

    My steps are not alone
In these bright walks ; the sweet south-west,
          at play,
Flies, rustling, where the painted leaves are
         strown
    Along the winding way.

    And far in heaven, the while,
The sun, that sends that gale to wander here,
Pours out on the fair earth his quiet smile,—
    The sweetest of the year.

    Where now the solemn shade,
Verdure and gloom where many branches meet ;
So grateful, when the noon of summer made
    The valleys sick with heat ?

Let in through all the trees
Come the strange rays ; the forest depths are
bright ;
Their sunny-colored foliage, in the breeze,
Twinkles, like beams of light.

The rivulet, late unseen,
Where bickering through the shrubs its waters
run,
Shines with the image of its golden screen
And glimmerings of the sun.

But,'neath yon crimson tree,
Lover to listening maid might breathe his flame,
Nor mark, within its roseate canopy,
Her blush of maiden shame.

Oh, Autumn ! why so soon
Depart the hues that make thy forests glad,
Thy gentle wind and thy fair sunny noon,
And leave thee wild and sad ?

Ah ! 'twere a lot too blest
For ever in thy colored shades to stray ;
Amid the kisses of the soft south-west
    To rove and dream for aye ;

    And leave the vain low strife
That makes men mad—the tug for wealth and
           power,
The passions and the cares that wither life,
    And waste its little hour.

MUTATION.

They talk of short-lived pleasure—be it so—
  Pain dies as quickly : stern, hard-featured
        pain
Expires, and lets her weary prisoner go.
  The fiercest agonies have shortest reign ;
  And after dreams of horror, comes again
The welcome morning with its rays of peace.
  Oblivion, softly wiping out the stain,
Makes the strong secret pangs of shame to cease :
Remorse is virtue's root ; its fair increase
  Are fruits of innocence and blessedness.

Thus joy, o'erborne and bound, doth still release
 His young limbs from the chains that round
      him press.
Weep not that the world changes—did it keep
A stable, changeless state, 'twere cause indeed
      to weep.

NOVEMBER.

YET one smile more, departing, distant sun !
  One mellow smile through the soft vapory air,
Ere, o'er the frozen earth, the loud winds run,
  Or snows are sifted o'er the meadows bare.
One smile on the brown hills and naked trees,
    And the dark rocks whose summer wreaths
        are cast,
And the blue gentian flower, that, in the breeze,
  Nods lonely, of her beauteous race the last.
Yet a few sunny days, in which the bee

Shall murmur by the hedge that skirts the
way,
The cricket chirp upon the russet lea,
And man delight to linger in thy ray.
Yet one rich smile, and we will try to bear
The piercing winter frost, and winds, and dark-
ened air.

SONG OF THE GREEK AMAZON.

I BUCKLE to my slender side
   The pistol and the scimitar,
And in my maiden flower and pride
   Am come to share the tasks of war.
And yonder stands my fiery steed,
   That paws the ground and neighs to go,
My charger of the Arab breed,—
   I took him from the routed foe.

My mirror is the mountain spring,
   At which I dress my ruffled hair ;

My dimmed and dusty arms I bring,
   And wash away the blood-stain there.
Why should I guard from wind and sun
   This cheek, whose virgin rose is fled ?
It was for one—oh, only one—
   I kept its bloom, and he is dead.

But they who slew him—unaware
   Of coward murderers lurking nigh—
And left him to the fowls of air,
   Are yet alive—and they must die.
They slew him—and my virgin years
   Are vowed to Greece and vengeance now,
And many an Othman dame in tears,
   Shall rue the Grecian maiden's vow.

I touched the lute in better days,
   I led in dance the joyous band ;
Ah ! they may move to mirthful lays
   Whose hands can touch a lover's hand.

The march of hosts that haste to meet
    Seems gayer than the dance to me ;
The lute's sweet tones are not so sweet
    As the fierce shout of victory.

TO A CLOUD.

Beautiful cloud ! with folds so soft and fair,
  Swimming in the pure quiet air !
Thy fleeces bathed in sunlight, while below
  Thy shadow o'er the vale moves slow ;
Where, midst their labor, pause the reaper train,
  As cool it comes along the grain.
Beautiful cloud ! I would I were with thee
  In thy calm way o'er land and sea :
To rest on thy unrolling skirts, and look
  On Earth as on an open book ;

On streams that tie her realms with silver bands,
   And the long ways that seam her lands ;
And hear her humming cities, and the sound
   Of the great ocean breaking round.
Ay—I would sail, upon thy air-borne car,
   To blooming regions distant far,
To where the sun of Andalusia shines
   On his own olive-groves and vines,
Or the soft lights of Italy's clear sky
   In smiles upon her ruins lie.

But I would woo the winds to let us rest
   O'er Greece long fettered and oppressed,
Whose sons at length have heard the call that
       comes
   From the old battle-fields and tombs,
And risen, and drawn the sword, and on the foe
   Have dealt the swift and desperate blow,
And the Othman power is cloven, and the stroke
   Has touched its chains, and they are broke.

Ay, we would linger till the sunset there
  Should come, to purple all the air,
And thou reflect upon the sacred ground
  The ruddy radiance streaming round.

Bright meteor ! for the summer noontide made !
  Thy peerless beauty yet shall fade.
The sun, that fills with light each glistening fold,
  Shall set, and leave thee dark and cold.
The blast shalt rend thy skirts, or thou mayst
        frown
  In the dark heaven when storms come down,
And weep in rain till man's inquiring eye
  Miss thee, for ever, from the sky.

THE MURDERED TRAVELLER.

WHEN spring, to woods and wastes around,
  Brought bloom and joy again,
The murdered traveller's bones were found,
  Far down a narrow glen.

The fragrant birch, above him, hung
  Her tassels in the sky ;
And many a vernal blossom sprung,
  And nodded careless by.

The red-bird warbled, as he wrought
　　His hanging nest o'erhead,
And fearless, near the fatal spot,
　　Her young the partridge led.

But there was weeping far away,
　　And gentle eyes for him,
With watching many an anxious day,
　　Were sorrowful and dim.

They little knew, who loved him so,
　　The fearful death he met,
When shouting o'er the desert snow,
　　Unarmed, and hard beset ;—

Nor how, when round the frosty pole
　　The northern dawn was red,
The mountain wolf and wild cat stole
　　To banquet on the dead ;—

Nor how, when strangers found his bones,
  They dressed the hasty bier,
And marked his grave with nameless stones,
  Unmoistened by a tear.

But long they looked, and feared, and wept,
  Within his distant home ;
And dreamed, and started as they slept,
  For joy that he was come.

Long, long they looked—but never spied
  His welcome step again,
Nor knew the fearful death he died
  Far down that narrow glen.

HYMN TO THE NORTH STAR.

THE sad and solemn night
Hath yet her multitude of cheerful fires ;
   The glorious host of light
Walk the dark hemisphere till she retires ;
All through her silent watches, gliding slow,
Her constellations come, and climb the heavens,
     and go.

   Day, too, hath many a star
To grace his gorgeous reign, as bright as they ;
   Through the blue fields afar,

Unseen, they follow in his flaming way :
Many a bright lingerer, as the eve grows dim,
Tells what a radiant troop arose and set with
    him.

    And thou dost see them rise,
Star of the Pole ! and thou dost see them set.
    Alone, in thy cold skies,
Thou keep'st thy old unmoving station yet,
Nor join'st the dances of that glittering train,
Nor dipp'st thy virgin orb in the blue western
    main.

    There, at morn's rosy birth,
Thou lookest meekly through the kindling air,
    And eve, that round the earth
Chases the day, beholds thee watching there ;
There noontide finds thee, and the hour that calls
The shapes of polar flame to scale heaven's
    azure walls.

Alike, beneath thine eye,
The deeds of darkness and of light are done ;
　　High towards the star-lit sky
Towns blaze, the smoke of battle blots the sun,
The night-storm on a thousand hills is loud,
And the strong wind of day doth mingle sea
　　　and cloud.

　　On thine unaltering blaze,
The half-wrecked mariner, his compass lost,
　　Fixes his steady gaze,
And steers, undoubting, to the friendly coast ;
And they who stray in perilous wastes, by night,
Are glad when thou dost shine to guide their
　　　footsteps right.

　　And, therefore, bards of old,
Sages, and hermits of the solemn wood,
　　Did in thy beams behold

A beauteous type of that unchanging good,
That bright eternal beacon, by whose ray
The voyager of time should shape his heedful
        way.

THE LAPSE OF TIME.

Lament who will, in fruitless tears,
 The speed with which our moments fly
I sigh not over vanished years,
 But watch the years that hasten by.

Look, how they come,—a mingled crowd
 Of bright and dark, but rapid days;
Beneath them, like a summer cloud,
 The wide world changes as I gaze.

What ! grieve that time has brought so soon
   The sober age of manhood on ?
As idly might I weep at noon,
   To see the blush of morning gone.

Could I give up the hopes that glow
   In prospect like Elysian isles ;
And let the cheerful future go,
   With all her promises and smiles ?

The future !—cruel were the power
   Whose doom would tear thee from my heart
Thou sweetener of the present hour !
   We cannot—no—we will not part.

Oh, leave me, still, the rapid flight
   That makes the changing seasons gay,
The grateful speed that brings the night,
   The swift and glad return of day ;

The months that touch, with added grace,
  This little prattler at my knee,
In whose arch eye and speaking face
  New meaning every hour I see ;

The years, that o'er each sister land
  Shall lift the country of my birth,
And nurse her strength, till she shall stand
  The pride and pattern of the earth :

Till younger commonwealths, for aid,
  Shall cling about her ample robe,
And from her frown shall shrink afraid
  The crowned oppressors of the globe.

True—time will seam and blanch my brow—
  Well—I shall sit with aged men,
And my good glass will tell me how
  A grizzly beard becomes me then.

And then, should no dishonor lie
   Upon my head, when I am gray,
Love yet shall watch my fading eye,
   And smooth the path of my decay.

Then haste thee, Time—'tis kindness all
   That speeds thy winged feet so fast ;
Thy pleasures stay not till they pall,
   And all thy pains are quickly past.

Thou fliest and bear'st away our woes,
   And as thy shadowy train depart,
The memory of sorrow grows
   A lighter burden on the heart.

SONG OF THE STARS.

WHEN the radiant morn of creation broke,
And the world in the smile of God awoke,
And the empty realms of darkness and death
Were moved through their depths by his mighty
       breath,
And orbs of beauty and spheres of flame
From the void abyss by myriads came,—
In the joy of youth as they darted away,
Through the widening wastes of space to play,
Their silver voices in chorus rang,
And· this was the song the bright ones sang:

" Away, away, through the wide, wide sky,
The blue fair fields that before us lie,—
Each sun with the worlds that round him roll,
Each planet, poised on her turning pole ;
With her isles of green, and her clouds of white,
And her waters that lie like fluid light.

" For the source of glory uncovers his face,
And the brightness o'erflows unbounded space ;
And we drink as we go the luminous tides
In our ruddy air and our blooming sides ;
Lo, yonder the living splendors play ;
Away, on our joyous path, away !

" Look, look, through our glittering ranks afar,
In the infinite azure, star after star,
How they brighten and bloom as they swiftly
          pass !
How the verdure runs o'er each rolling mass !

And the path of the gentle winds is seen,
Where the small waves dance, and the young
     woods lean.

" And see, where the brighter day-beams pour,
How the rainbows hang in the sunny shower ;
And the morn and eve, with their pomp of hues,
Shift o'er the bright planets and shed their dews;
And 'twixt them both, o'er the teeming ground,
With her shadowy cone the night goes round !

" Away, away ! in our blossoming bowers,
In the soft air wrapping these spheres of ours,
In the seas and fountains that shine with morn,
See, Love is brooding, and Life is born,
And breathing myriads are breaking from night,
To rejoice, like us, in motion and light.

" Glide on in your beauty, ye youthful spheres,
To weave the dance that measures the years ;
    Vol. I.—8

Glide on, in the glory and gladness sent,
To the furthest wall of the firmament,—
The boundless visible smile of Him,
To the veil of whose brow your lamps are dim."

A FOREST HYMN.

THE groves were God's first temples. Ere
     man learned
To hew the shaft, and lay the architrave,
And spread the roof above them,—ere he framed
The lofty vault, to gather and roll back
The sound of anthems ; in the darkling wood,
Amid the cool and silence, he knelt down,
And offered to the Mightiest solemn thanks
And supplication. For his simple heart
Might not resist the sacred influences

Which, from the stilly twilight of the place,
And from the gray old trunks that high in heaven
Mingled their mossy boughs, and from the sound
Of the invisible breath that swayed at once
All their green tops, stole over him, and bowed
His spirit with the thought of boundless power
And inaccessible majesty.   Ah, why
Should we, in the world's riper years, neglect
God's ancient sanctuaries, and adore
Only among the crowd, and under roofs
That our frail hands have raised?   Let me, at
          least,
Here, in the shadow of this aged wood,
Offer one hymn—thrice happy, if it find
Acceptance in His ear.

                    Father, thy hand
Hath reared these venerable columns, thou
Didst weave this verdant roof.   Thou didst look
          down

Upon the naked earth, and, forthwith, rose
All these fair ranks of trees.   They, in thy sun,
Budded, and shook their green leaves in thy
      breeze,
And shot towards heaven.   The century-living
      crow,
Whose birth was in their tops, grew old and died
Among their branches, till, at last, they stood,
As now they stand, massy, and tall, and dark,
Fit shrine for humble worshipper to hold
Communion with his Maker. These dim vaults,
These winding aisles, of human pomp or pride
Report not.   No fantastic carvings show
The boast of our vain race to change the form
Of thy fair works.   But thou art here—thou
      fill'st
The solitude.   Thou art in the soft winds
That run along the summit of these trees
In music ; thou art in the cooler breath
That from the inmost darkness of the place

Comes, scarcely felt ; the barky trunks, the
     ground,
The fresh moist ground, are all instinct with
     thee.
Here is continual worship ;—nature, here,
In the tranquillity that thou dost love,
Enjoys thy presence.   Noiselessly, around,
From perch to perch, the solitary bird
Passes ; and yon clear spring, that, midst its
     herbs,
Wells softly forth and wandering steeps the roots
Of half the mighty forest, tells no tale
Of all the good it does.   Thou hast not left
Thyself without a witness, in these shades,
Of thy perfections.   Grandeur, strength, and
     grace
Are here to speak of thee.   This mighty oak—
By whose immovable stem I stand and seem
Almost annihilated—not a prince,
In all that proud old world beyond the deep,

E'er wore his crown as loftily as he
Wears the green coronal of leaves with which
Thy hand has graced him.   Nestled at his root
Is beauty, such as blooms not in the glare
Of the broad sun.   That delicate forest flower
With scented breath, and look so like a smile,
Seems, as it issues from the shapeless mould,
An emanation of the indwelling Life,
A visible token of the upholding Love,
That are the soul of this wide universe.

My heart is awed within me when I think
Of the great miracle that still goes on,
In silence, round me—the perpetual work
Of thy creation, finished, yet renewed
For ever.   Written on thy works I read
The lesson of thy own eternity.
Lo ! all grow old and die—but see again
How on the faltering footsteps of decay

Youth presses—ever gay and beautiful youth,
In all its beautiful forms.   These lofty trees
Wave not less proudly that their ancestors
Moulder beneath them.   Oh, there is not lost
One of earth's charms : upon her bosom yet,
After the flight of untold centuries,
The freshness of her far beginning lies
And yet shall lie.   Life mocks the idle hate
Of his arch enemy Death—yea, seats himself
Upon the tyrant's throne—the sepulchre,
And of the triumphs of his ghastly foe
Makes his own nourishment. For he came forth
From thine own bosom, and shall have no end.

There have been holy men who hid themselves
Deep in the woody wilderness, and gave
Their lives to thought and prayer, till they
          outlived
The generation born with them, nor seemed
Less aged than the hoary trees and rocks

Around them ;—and there have been holy men
Who deemed it were not well to pass life thus.
But let me often to these solitudes
Retire, and in thy presence reassure
My feeble virtue. Here its enemies,
The passions, at thy plainer footsteps shrink
And tremble and are still. Oh, God! when thou
Dost scare the world with tempests, set on fire
The heavens with falling thunderbolts, or fill
With all the waters of the firmament,
The swift dark whirlwind that uproots the woods
And drowns the villages ; when, at thy call,
Uprises the great deep and throws himself
Upon the continent, and overwhelms
Its cities—who forgets not, at the sight
Of these tremendous tokens of thy power,
His pride, and lays his strifes and follies by ?
Oh, from these sterner aspects of thy face
Spare me and mine, nor let us need the wrath

Of the mad unchained elements to teach
Who rules them.   Be it ours to meditate,
In these calm shades, thy milder majesty,
And to the beantiful order of thy works
Learn to conform the order of our lives.

"OH, FAIREST OF THE RURAL MAIDS."

Oh, fairest of the rural maids !
Thy birth was in the forest shades ;
Green boughs, and glimpses of the sky,
Were all that met thine infant eye.

Thy sports, thy wanderings, when a child,
Were ever in the sylvan wild ;
And all the beauty of the place
Is in thy heart and on thy face.

The twilight of the trees and rocks
Is in the light shade of thy locks ;
Thy step is as the wind, that weaves
Its playful way among the leaves.

Thine eyes are springs, in whose serene
And silent waters heaven is seen ;
Their lashes are the herbs that look
On their young figures in the brook.

The forest depths, by foot unpressed,
Are not more sinless than thy breast ;
The holy peace, that fills the air
Of those calm solitudes, is there.

"I BROKE THE SPELL THAT HELD ME LONG."

I BROKE the spell that held me long,
The dear, dear witchery of song.
I said, the poet's idle lore
Shall waste my prime of years no more,
For Poetry, though heavenly born,
Consorts with poverty and scorn.

I broke the spell—nor deemed its power
Could fetter me another hour.
Ah, thoughtless! how could I forget
Its causes were around me yet?

For wheresoe'er I looked, the while,
Was nature's everlasting smile.

Still came and lingered on my sight
Of flowers and streams the bloom and light,
And glory of the stars and sun ;—
And these and poetry are one.
They, ere the world had held me long,
Recalled me to the love of song.

JUNE.

I GAZED upon the glorious sky
 And the green mountains round,
And thought that when I came to lie
 At rest within the ground,
'Twere pleasant, that in flowery June,
When brooks send up a cheerful tune,
 And groves a joyous sound,
The sexton's hand, my grave to make,
The rich, green mountain turf should break.

A cell within the frozen mould,
 A coffin borne through sleet,

And icy clods above it rolled,
 While fierce the tempests beat—
Away !—I will not think of these—
Blue be the sky and soft the breeze,
 Earth green beneath the feet,
And be the damp mould gently pressed
Into my narrow place of rest.

There, through the long, long summer hours,
 The golden light should lie,
And thick young herbs and groups of flowers
 Stand in their beauty by.
The oriole should build and tell
His love-tale close beside my cell ;
 The idle butterfly
Should rest him there, and there be heard
The housewife bee and humming-bird.

And what if cheerful shouts at noon
 Come, from the village sent,

Or songs of maids, beneath the moon,
  With fairy laughter blent ?
And what if, in the evening light,
Betrothed lovers walk in sight
  Of my low monument ?
I would the lovely scene around
Might know no sadder sight or sound

I know, I know I should not see
  The season's glorious show,
Nor would its brightness shine for me,
  Nor its wild music flow ;
But if, around my place of sleep,
The friends I love should come to weep,
  They might not haste to go.
Soft airs and song and light and bloom
Should keep them lingering by my tomb.

These to their softened hearts should bear
  The thought of what has been,

And speak of one who cannot share
    The gladness of the scene ;
Whose part, in all the pomp that fills
The circuit of the summer hills,
    Is—that his grave is green :
And deeply would their hearts rejoice
To hear again his living voice.

A SONG OF PITCAIRN'S ISLAND.

Come, take our boy, and we will go
  Before our cabin door ;
The winds shall bring us, as they blow,
  The murmurs of the shore ;
And we will kiss his young blue eyes,
And I will sing him, as he lies,
  Songs that were made of yore :
I'll sing, in his delighted ear,
The island lays thou lov'st to hear.

And thou, while stammering I repeat,
  Thy country's tongue shall teach ;

'Tis not so soft, but far more sweet
    Than my own native speech :
For thou no other tongue didst know,
When, scarcely twenty moons ago,
    Upon Tahete's beach,
Thou cam'st to woo me to be thine,
With many a speaking look and sign.

I knew thy meaning—thou didst praise
    My eyes, my locks of jet ;
Ah ! well for me they won thy gaze—
    But thine were fairer yet !
I'm glad to see my infant wear
Thy soft blue eyes and sunny hair,
    And when my sight is met
By his white brow and blooming cheek,
I feel a joy I cannot speak.

Come talk of Europe's maids with me,
    Whose necks and cheeks, they tell,

Outshine the beauty of the sea,
    White foam and crimson shell.
I'll shape like theirs my simple dress,
And bind like them each jetty tress,
    A sight to please thee well ;
And for my dusky brow will braid
A bonnet like an English maid.

Come, for the soft low sunlight calls,
    We lose the pleasant hours ;
'Tis lovelier than these cottage walls,—
    That seat among the flowers.
And I will learn of thee a prayer
To Him who gave a home so fair,
    A lot so blest as ours—
The God who made for thee and me
This sweet lone isle amid the sea.

THE FIRMAMENT.

Ay ! gloriously thou standest there,
   Beautiful, boundless firmament !
That, swelling wide o'er earth and air,
   And round the horizon bent,
With thy bright vault, and sapphire wall,
Dost overhang and circle all.

Far, far below thee, tall gray trees
   Arise, and piles built up of old,

And hills, whose ancient summits freeze
  In the fierce light and cold.
The eagle soars his utmost height,
Yet far thou stretchest o'er his flight.

Thou hast thy frowns—with thee on high
  The storm has made his airy seat.
Beyond that soft blue curtain lie
  His stores of hail and sleet.
Thence the consuming lightnings break,
There the strong hurricanes awake.

Yet art thou prodigal of smiles—
  Smiles, sweeter than thy frowns are stern.
Earth sends, from all her thousand isles,
  A shout at their return.
The glory that comes down from thee,
Bathes, in deep joy, the land and sea.

The sun, the gorgeous sun is thine,
   The pomp that brings and shuts the day,
The clouds that round him change and shine,
   The airs that fan his way.
Thence look the thoughtful stars, and there
The meek moon walks the silent air.

The sunny Italy may boast
   The beauteous tints that flush her skies,
And lovely, round the Grecian coast,
   May thy blue pillars rise.
I only know how fair they stand
Around my own beloved land.

And they are fair—a charm is theirs,
   That earth, the proud green earth, has not—
With all the forms, and hues, and airs,
   That haunt her sweetest spot.
We gaze upon thy calm pure sphere.
And read of Heaven's eternal year.

Oh, when, amid the throng of men,
The heart grows sick of hollow mirth,
How willingly we turn us then
Away from this cold earth,
And look into thy azure breast,
For seats of innocence and rest !

"I CANNOT FORGET WITH WHAT FERVID DEVOTION."

I CANNOT forget with what fervid devotion
   I worshipped the visions of verse and of fame:
Each gaze at the glories of earth, sky, and
       ocean,
   To my kindled emotions, was wind over flame.

And deep were my musings in life's early blos-
       som,
   Mid the twilight of mountain groves wander-
       ing long ;

How thrilled my young veins, and how throbbed
    my full bosom,
  When o'er me descended the spirit of song.

'Mong the deep-cloven fells that for ages had
    listened
  To the rush of the pebble-paved river between,
Where the kingfisher screamed and gray preci-
    pice glistened,
  All breathless with awe have I gazed on the
    scene ;

Till I felt the dark power o'er my reveries steal-
    ing,
  From the gloom of the thickets that over me
    hung,
And the thoughts that awoke in that rapture
    of feeling,
  Were formed into verse as they rose to my
    tongue.

Bright visions ! I mixed with the world, and
    ye faded ;
  No longer your pure rural worshipper now ;
In the haunts your continual presence pervaded,
    Ye shrink from the signet of care on my brow.

In the old mossy groves on the breast of the
    mountain,
  In deep lonely glens where the waters com-
    plain,
By the shade of the rock, by the gush of the
    fountain,
  I seek your loved footsteps, but seek them in
    vain.

Oh, leave not, forlorn and for ever forsaken,
  Your pupil and victim to life and its tears !
But sometimes return, and in mercy awaken
  The glories ye showed to his earlier years.

TO A MUSQUITO.

Fair insect ! that, with threadlike legs spread
      out,
  And blood-extracting bill and filmy wing,
Dost murmur, as thou slowly sail'st about,
  In pitiless ears full many a plaintive thing,
And tell how little our large veins should bleed,
Would we but yield them to thy bitter need.

Unwillingly, I own, and, what is worse,
  Full angrily men hearken to thy plaint ;

Thou gettest many a brush and many a curse,
　For saying thou art gaunt, and starved, and
　　　faint :
Even the old beggar, while he asks for food,
Would kill thee, hapless stranger, if he could.

I call thee stranger, for the town, I ween,
　Has not the honor of so proud a birth,—
Thou com'st from Jersey meadows, fresh and
　　　green,
　　The offspring of the gods, though born on
　　　earth ;
For Titan was thy sire, and fair was she,
The ocean nymph that nursed thy infancy.

Beneath the rushes was thy cradle swung,
　And when, at length, thy gauzy wings grew
　　　strong,
　Abroad to gentle airs their folds were flung,
　　Rose in the sky and bore.thee soft along ;

The south wind breathed to waft thee on thy
    way,
And danced and shone beneath the billowy bay.

Calm rose afar the city spires, and thence
   Came the deep murmur of its throng of men,
And as its grateful odors met thy sense,
   They seemed the perfumes of thy native fen.
Fair lay its crowded streets, and at the sight
Thy tiny song grew shriller with delight.

At length thy pinions fluttered in Broadway—
   Ah, there were fairy steps, and white necks
      kissed
By wanton airs, and eyes whose killing ray
   Shone through the snowy veils like stars
      through mist ;
And fresh as morn, on many a cheek and chin,
Bloomed the bright blood through the trans-
      parent skin.

Sure these were sights to touch an anchorite !
    What ! do I hear thy slender voice complain?
Thou wailest, when I talk of beauty's light,
    As if it brought the memory of pain.
Thou art a wayward being—well—come near,
And pour thy tale of sorrow in my ear.

What sayst thou—slanderer !—rouge makes
            thee sick ?
    And China bloom at best is sorry food ?
And Rowland's Kalydor, if laid on thick,
    Poisons the thirsty wretch that bores for
            blood ?
Go ! 'twas a just reward that met thy crime—
But shun the sacrilege another time.

That bloom was made to look at, not to touch ;
    To worship, not approach, that radiant white ;
And well might sudden vengeance light on such

As dared, like thee, most impiously to bite.
Thou shouldst have gazed at distance and ad-
    mired,
Murmured thy adoration and retired.

Thou'rt welcome to the town—but why come
        here
    To bleed a brother poet, gaunt like thee?
Alas! the little blood I have is dear,
    And thin will be the banquet drawn from me.
Look round—the pale-eyed sisters in my cell,
Thy old acquaintance, Song and Famine, dwell.

Try some plump alderman, and suck the blood
    Enriched by generous wine and costly meat;
On well-filled skins, sleek as thy native mud,
    Fix thy light pump and press thy freckled
        feet:
Go to the men for whom, in ocean's halls,
The oyster breeds, and the green turtle sprawls.

There corks are drawn, and the red vintage
         flows
  To fill the swelling veins for thee, and now
The ruddy cheek and now the ruddier nose
    Shall tempt thee, as thou flittest round the
         brow ;
And when the hour of sleep its quiet brings,
No angry hand shall rise to brush thy wings.

LINES ON REVISITING THE COUNTRY.

I STAND upon my native hills again,
    Broad, round, and green, that in the summer
        sky
With garniture of waving grass and grain,
    Orchards, and beechen forests, basking lie;
While deep the sunless glens are scooped be-
        tween,
Where brawl o'er shallow beds the streams un-
        seen.

A lisping voice and glancing eyes are near,
    And ever restless feet of one, who, now,

Gathers the blossoms of her fourth bright year ;
  There plays a gladness o'er her fair young
      brow,
As breaks the varied scene upon her sight,
Upheaved and spread in verdure and in light.

For I have taught her, with delighted eye,
  To gaze upon the mountains,—to behold,
With deep affection, the pure ample sk ,
  And clouds along its blue abysses rolled,—
To love the song of waters, and to hear
The melody of winds with charmed ear.

Here, I have 'scaped the city's stifling heat,
  Its horrid sounds and its polluted air ;
And, where the season's milder fervors beat,
  And gales, that sweep the forest borders, bear
The song of bird, and sound of running stream,
Am come awhile to wander and to dream.

Ay, flame thy fiercest, sun ! thou canst not
wake,
In this pure air, the plague that walks unseen.
The maize leaf and the maple bough but take,
From thy strong heats, a deeper, glossier
green.
The mountain wind, that faints not in thy ray,
Sweeps the blue steams of pestilence away.

The mountain wind ! most spiritual thing of all
The wide earth knows ; when, in the sultry
time,
He stoops him from his vast cerulean hall,
He seems the breath of a celestial clime !
As if from heaven's wide-open gates did flow
Health and refreshment on the world below.

THE DEATH OF THE FLOWERS.

THE melancholy days are come, the saddest of
     the year,
Of wailing winds, and naked woods, and mead-
     ows brown and sere.
Heaped in the hollows of the grove, the autumn
     leaves lie dead ;
They rustle to the eddying gust, and to the rab-
     bit's tread.
The robin and the wren are flown, and from the
     shrubs the jay,
And from the wood-top calls the crow through
     all the gloomy day.

Where are the flowers, the fair young flowers,
    that lately sprang and stood
In brighter light, and softer airs, a beauteous
    sisterhood ?
Alas ! they all are in their graves, the gentle
    race of flowers
Are lying in their lowly beds, with the fair and
    good of ours.
The rain is falling where they lie, but the cold
    November rain
Calls not from out the gloomy earth the lovely
    ones again.

The wind-flower and the violet, they perished
    long ago,
And the brier-rose and the orchis died amid the
    summer glow ;
But on the hill the golden-rod, and the aster in
    the wood,

And the yellow sun-flower by the brook in au-
    tumn beauty stood,
Till fell the frost from the clear cold heaven,
    as falls the plague on men,
And the brightness of their smile was gone,
    from upland, glade, and glen.

And now, when comes the calm mild day, as
    still such days will come,
To call the squirrel and the bee from out their
    winter home ;
When the sound of dropping nuts is heard,
    though all the trees are still,
And twinkle in the smoky light the waters of
    the rill,
The south wind searches for the flowers whose
    fragrance late he bore,
And sighs to find them in the wood and by the
    stream no more.

And then I think of one who in her youthful
    beauty died,
The fair meek blossom that grew up and faded
    by my side :
In the cold moist earth we laid her, when the
    forest cast the leaf,
And we wept that one so lovely should have a
    life so brief :
Yet not unmeet it was that one, like that
    young friend of ours,
So gentle and so beautiful, should perish with
    the flowers.

ROMERO.

When freedom, from the land of Spain,
   By Spain's degenerate sons was driven,
Who gave their willing limbs again
   To wear the chain so lately riven ;
Romero broke the sword he wore—
   " Go, faithful brand," the warrior said,
" Go, undishonored, never more
   The blood of man shall make thee red :
   I grieve for that already shed ;
And I am sick at heart to know,
That faithful friend and noble foe

Have only bled to make more strong
The yoke that Spain has worn so long.
Wear it who will, in abject fear—
   I wear it not who have been free ;
The perjured Ferdinand shall hear
   No oath of loyalty from me."
Then, hunted by the hounds of power,
   Romero chose a safe retreat,
Where bleak Nevada's summits tower
   Above the beauty at their feet.
There once, when on his cabin lay
The crimson light of setting day,
When even on the mountain's breast
The chainless winds were all at rest,
And he could hear the river's flow
From the calm paradise below ;
Warmed with his former fires again,
He framed this rude but solemn strain :

I.

" Here will I make my home—for here at
    least I see
Upon this wild Sierra's side, the steps of
    Liberty.
Where the locust chirps unscared beneath the
    unpruned lime,
And the merry bee doth hide from man the
    spoil of the mountain thyme ;
Where the pure winds come and go, and the
    wild vine strays at will,
An outcast from the haunts of men, she dwells
    with Nature still.

II.

" I see the valleys, Spain ! where thy mighty
    rivers run,
And the hills that lift thy harvests and vine-
    yards to the sun,

And the flocks that drink thy brooks and
    sprinkle all the green.
Where lie thy plains, with sheep-walks seamed,
    and olive-shades between.
I see thy fig-trees bask, with the fair pome-
    granate near,
And the fragrance of thy lemon-groves can
    almost reach me here.

III.

"Fair—fair—but fallen Spain ! 'tis with a
    swelling heart,
That I think on all thou mightst have been,
    and look at what thou art ;
But the strife is over now, and all the good and
    brave,
That would have raised thee up, are gone, to
    exile or the grave.

Thy fleeces are for monks, thy grapes for the
    convent feast,
And the wealth of all thy harvest fields for the
    pampered lord and priest.

IV.

    " But I shall see the day—it will come before
        I die—
I shall see it in my silver hairs, and with an age-
        dimmed eye ;—
When the spirit of the land to liberty shall
        bound,
As yonder fountain leaps away from the dark-
        ness of the ground ;
And to my mountain cell, the voices of the free
Shall rise, as from the beaten shore the thunders
        of the sea."

A MEDITATION ON RHODE ISLAND COAL.

Decolor, obscuris, vilis, non ille repexam
Cesariem regum, non candida virginis ornat
Colla, nec insigni splendet per cingula morsu.
Sed nova si nigri videas miracula saxi,
Tunc superat pulchros cultus et quicquid Eois
Indus litoribus rubrâ scrutatur in algâ.

CLAUDIAN.

I SAT beside the glowing grate, fresh heaped
    With Newport coal, and as the flame grew
        bright
—The many-colored flame—and played and
        leaped,

I thought of rainbows and the northern light,
Moore's Lalla Rookh, the Treasury Report,
And other brilliant matters of the sort.

And last I thought of that fair isle which sent
    The mineral fuel ; on a summer day
I saw it once, with heat and travel spent,
    And scratched by dwarf'oaks in the hollow
        way ;
Now dragged through sand, now jolted over
        stone—
A rugged road through rugged Tiverton.

And hotter grew the air, and hollower grew
    The deep-worn path, and horror-struck, I
        thought,
Where will this dreary passage lead me to ?
    This long dull road, so narrow, deep, and hot ?
I looked to see it dive in earth outright ;
I looked—but saw a far more welcome sight.

Like a soft mist upon the evening shore,
　　At once a lovely isle before me lay,
Smooth and with tender verdure covered o'er,
　　As if just risen from its calm inland bay ;
Sloped each way gently to the grassy edge,
And the small waves that dallied with the sedge.

The barley was just reaped—its heavy sheaves
　　Lay on the stubble field—the tall maize stood
Dark in its summer growth, and shook its
　　　　leaves—
　　And bright the sunlight played on the young
　　　　wood—
For fifty years ago, the old men say,
The Briton hewed their ancient groves away.

I saw where fountains freshened the green land,
　　And where the pleasant road, from door to
　　　　door,
With rows of cherry-trees on either hand,

Went wandering all that fertile region o'er—
Rogue's Island once—but when the rogues were
    dead,
Rhode Island was the name it took instead.

Beautiful island ! then it only seemed
    A lovely stranger—it has grown a friend.
I gazed on its smooth slopes, but never dreamed
    How soon that green and quiet isle would
    send
The treasures of its womb across the sea,
To warm a poet's room, and boil his tea.

Dark anthracite ! that reddenest on my hearth,
    Thou in those island mines didst slumber
    long ;
But now thou art come forth to move the earth,
    And put to shame the men that mean thee
    wrong.

Thou shalt be coals of fire to those that hate
    thee,
And warm the shins of all that underrate thee.

Yea, they did wrong thee foully—they who
    mocked
  Thy honest face, and said thou wouldst not
    burn ;
Of hewing thee to chimney pieces talked
  And grew profane—and swore in bitter scorn,
That men might to thy inner caves retire,
And there, unsinged, abide the day of fire.

Yet is thy greatness nigh. I pause to state,
  That I too have seen greatness—even I—
Shook hands with Adams—stared at La Fayette,
  When, barehead, in the hot noon of July,
He would not let the umbrella be held o'er him,
For which three cheers burst from the mob
    before him.

And I have seen—not many months ago—
   An eastern Governor in chapeau bras
And military coat, a glorious show !
   Ride forth to visit the reviews, and ah !
How oft he smiled and bowed to Jonathan !
How many hands were shook and votes were
       won !

'Twas a great Governor—thou too shalt be
   Great in thy turn—and wide shall spread thy
      fame,
And swiftly ; furthest Maine shall hear of thee,
   And cold New Brunswick gladden at thy
      name,
And, faintly through its sleets, the weeping isle
That sends the Boston folks their cod shall
      smile.

For thou shalt forge vast railways, and shalt heat
   The hissing rivers into steam, and drive

Huge masses from thy mines, on iron feet,
　　Walking their steady way, as if alive,
Northward, till everlasting ice besets thee,
And south as far as the grim Spaniard lets thee.

Thou shalt make mighty engines swim the sea,
　　Like its own monsters—boats that for a guinea
Will take a man to Havre—and shalt be
　　The moving soul of many a spinning-jenny,
And ply thy shuttles, till a bard can wear
As good a suit of broadcloth as the mayor.

Then we will laugh at winter when we hear
　　The grim old churl about our dwellings rave ;
Thou, from that " ruler of the inverted year,"
　　Shalt pluck the knotty sceptre Cowper gave,
And pull him from his sledge, and drag him in,
And melt the icicles from off his chin.

THE NEW MOON.

WHEN, as the garish day is done,
Heaven burns with the descended sun,
    'Tis passing sweet to mark,
Amid that flush of crimson light,
The new moon's modest bow grow bright,
    As earth and sky grow dark.

Few are the hearts too cold to feel
A thrill of gladness o'er them steal,
    When first the wandering eye

Sees faintly, in the evening blaze,
That glimmering curve of tender rays
    Just planted in the sky.

The sight of that young crescent brings
Thoughts of all fair and youthful things—
    The hopes of early years,
And childhood's purity and grace,
And joys that like a rainbow chase
    The passing shower of tears.

The captive yields him to the dream
Of freedom, when that virgin beam
    Comes out upon the air,
And painfully the sick man tries
To fix his dim and burning eyes
    On the soft promise there.

Most welcome to the lover's sight,
Glitters that pure, emerging light ;

For prattling poets say
That sweetest is the lovers' walk,
And tenderest is their murmured talk,
    Beneath its gentle ray.

And there do graver men behold
A type of errors, loved of old,
    Forsaken and forgiven ;
And thoughts and wishes not of earth,
Just opening in their early birth,
    Like that new light in heaven.

OCTOBER.

A SONNET.

Ay, thou art welcome, heaven's delicious breath,
  When woods begin to wear the crimson leaf,
  And suns grow meek, and the meek suns grow
      brief,
And the year smiles as it draws near its death.
Wind of the sunny south ! oh still delay
  In the gay woods and in the golden air,
  Like to a good old age released from care,
Journeying, in long serenity, away.
In such a bright, late quiet, would that I

Might wear out life like thee, mid bowers and
    brooks,
And, dearer yet, the sunshine of kind looks,
And music of kind voices ever nigh ;
And when my last sand twinkled in the glass,
Pass silently from men, as thou dost pass.

THE DAMSEL OF PERU.

WHERE olive leaves were twinkling in every
    wind that blew,
There sat beneath the pleasant shade a damsel
    of Peru.
Betwixt the slender boughs, as they opened to
    the air,
Came glimpses of her ivory neck and of her
    glossy hair ;
And sweetly rang her silver voice, within that
    shady nook,
As from the shrubby glen is heard the sound of
    hidden brook.

'Tis a song of love and valor, in the noble
    Spanish tongue,
That once upon the sunny plains of old Castile
    was sung ;
When, from their mountain holds, on the
    Moorish rout below,
Had rushed the Christians like a flood, and swept
    away the foe.
Awhile that melody is still, and then breaks
    forth anew,
A wilder rhyme, a livelier note, of freedom and
    Peru.

For she has bound the sword to a youthful
    lover's side,
And sent him to the war the day she should
    have been his bride,
And bade him bear a faithful heart to battle for
    the right,

And held the fountains of her eyes till he was
    out of sight.
Since the parting kiss was given, six weary
    months are fled,
And yet the foe is in the land, and blood must
    yet be shed.

A white hand parts the branches, a lovely face
    looks forth,
And bright dark eyes gaze steadfastly and
    sadly toward the north.
Thou look'st in vain, sweet maiden, the sharpest
    sight would fail
To spy a sign of human life abroad in all the
    vale ;
For the noon is coming on, and the sunbeams
    fiercely beat,
And the silent hills and forest-tops seem reeling
    in the heat.

That white hand is withdrawn, that fair sad
    face is gone,
But the music of that silver voice is flowing
    sweetly on,
Not as of late, in cheerful tones, but mournfully
    and low,—
A ballad of a tender maid heart-broken long
    ago,
Of him who died in battle, the youthful and the
    brave,
And her who died of sorrow, upon his early
    grave.

But see, along that mountain's slope, a fiery
    horseman ride ;
Mark his torn plume, his tarnished belt, the
    sabre at his side.
His spurs are buried rowel-deep, he rides with
    loosened rein,

There's blood upon his charger's flank, and foam
 upon the mane ;
He speeds him toward the olive-grove, along
 that shaded hill :
God shield the helpless maiden there, if he
 should mean her ill !

And suddenly that song has ceased, and suddenly
 I hear
A shriek sent up amid the shade, a shriek—but
 not of fear.
For tender accents follow, and tenderer pauses
 speak
The overflow of gladness, when words are all
 too weak :
"I lay my good sword at thy feet, for now Peru
 is free,
And I am come to dwell beside the olive-grove
 with thee."

THE AFRICAN CHIEF.

CHAINED in the market-place he stood,
  A man of giant frame,
Amid the gathering multitude
  That shrunk to hear his name—
All stern of look and strong of limb,
  His dark eye on the ground :—
And silently they gazed on him,
  As on a lion bound.

Vainly, but well, that chief had fought,
  He was a captive now,

Yet pride, that fortune humbles not,
  Was written on his brow.
The scars his dark broad bosom wore,
  Showed warrior true and brave ;
A prince among his tribe before,
  He could not be a slave.

Then to his conqueror he spake—
  " My brother is a king ;
Undo this necklace from my neck,
  And take this bracelet ring,
And send me where my brother reigns,
  And I will fill thy hands
With store of ivory from the plains,
  And gold-dust from the sands."

" Not for thy ivory nor thy gold
  Will I unbind thy chain ;
That bloody hand shall never hold
  The battle-spear again.

A price thy nation never gave
   Shall yet be paid for thee ;
For thou shalt be the Christian's slave,
   In lands beyond the sea."

Then wept the warrior chief and bade
   To shred his locks away ;
And one by one, each heavy braid
   Before the victor lay.
Thick were the platted locks, and long,
   And closely hidden there
Shone many a wedge of gold among
   The dark and crisped hair.

" Look, feast thy greedy eye with gold
   Long kept for sorest need :
Take it—thou askest sums untold,
   And say that I am freed.
Take it—my wife, the long, long day,
   Weeps by the cocoa-tree,

And my young children leave their play,
    And ask in vain for me."

" I take thy gold—but I have made
    Thy fetters fast and strong,
And ween that by the cocoa shade
    Thy wife will wait thee long."
Strong was the agony that shook
    The captive's frame to hear,
And the proud meaning of his look
    Was changed to mortal fear.

His heart was broken—crazed his brain ;
    At once his eye grew wild ;
He struggled fiercely with his chain,
    Whispered, and wept, and smiled ;
Yet wore not long those fatal bands
    And once, at shut of day,
They drew him forth upon the sands,
    The foul hyena's prey.

SPRING IN TOWN.

THE country ever has a lagging Spring,
   Waiting for May to call its violets forth,
And June its roses—showers and sunshine bring,
   Slowly, the deepening verdure o'er the earth;
To put their foliage out, the woods are slack,
And one by one the singing-birds come back.

Within the city's bounds the time of flowers
   Comes earlier.   Let a mild and sunny day,
Such as full often, for a few bright hours,

Breathes through the sky of March the airs
    of May,
Shine on our roofs and chase the wintry gloom—·
And lo ! our borders glow with sudden bloom.

For the wide sidewalks of Broadway are then
    Gorgeous as are a rivulet's banks in June,
That overhung with blossoms, through its glen,
    Slides soft away beneath the sunny noon,
And they who search the untrodden wood for
      flowers
Meet in its depths no lovelier ones than ours.

For here are eyes that shame the violet,
    Or the dark drop that on the pansy lies,
And foreheads, white, as when in clusters set,
    The anemones by forest fountains rise ;
And the spring-beauty boasts no tenderer streak
Than the soft red on many a youthful cheek.

And thick about those lovely temples lie
   Locks that the lucky Vignardonne has curled;
Thrice happy man ! whose trade it is to buy,
   And bake, and braid those love-nets of the
      world ;
Who curls of every glossy color keepest,
And sellest, it is said, the blackest cheapest.

And well thou mayst—for Italy's brown maids
   Send the dark locks with which their brows
      are dressed,
And Gascon lasses, from their jetty braids,
   Crop half, to buy a riband for the rest ;
But the fresh Norman girls their tresses spare,
And the Dutch damsel keeps her flaxen hair.

Then, henceforth, let no maid or matron grieve,
   To see her locks of an unlovely hue,
Frouzy or thin, for liberal art shall give
   Such piles of curls as nature never knew.

Eve, with her veil of tresses, at the sight
Had blushed, outdone, and owned herself a
     fright.

Soft voices and light laughter wake the street,
    Like notes of woodbirds, and where'er the
        eye
Threads the long way, plumes wave, and twin-
        kling feet
    Fall light, as hastes that crowd of beauty by.
The ostrich, hurrying o'er the desert space,
Scarce bore those tossing plumes with fleeter
        pace.

No swimming Juno-gait, of languor born,
    Is theirs, but a light step of freest grace,
Light as Camilla's o'er the unbent corn,—
    A step that speaks the spirit of the place,
Since Quiet, meek old dame, was driven away
To Sing-Sing and the shores of Tappan bay.

Ye that dash by in chariots ! who will care
　　For steeds or footmen now ? ye cannot show
Fair face, and dazzling dress, and graceful air,
　　And last edition of the shape !   Ah no ;
These sights are for the earth and open sky,
And your loud wheels unheeded rattle by.

THE GLADNESS OF NATURE.

Is this a time to be cloudy and sad,
   When our mother Nature laughs around ;
When even the deep blue heavens look glad,
   And gladness breathes from the blossoming
      ground ?

There are notes of joy from the hang-bird and
      wren,
   And the gossip of swallows through all the
      sky ;
The ground-squirrel gayly chirps by his der
   And the wilding bee hums merrily by.

The clouds are at play in the azure space,
 And their shadows at play on the bright
  green vale,
And here they stretch to the frolic chase,
 And there they roll on the easy gale.

There's a dance of leaves in that aspen bower,
 There's a titter of winds in that beechen tree,
There's a smile on the fruit and a smile on the
  flower,
 And a laugh from the brook that runs to the
  sea.

And look at the broad-faced sun, how he smiles
 On the dewy earth that smiles in his ray,
On the leaping waters and gay young isles ;
 Ay, look, and he'll smile thy gloom away.

THE DISINTERRED WARRIOR.

Gather him to his grave again,
   And solemnly and softly lay,
Beneath the verdure of the plain,
   The warrior's scattered bones away.
Pay the deep reverence, taught of old,
   The homage of man's heart to death ;
Nor dare to trifle with the mould
   Once hallowed by the Almighty's breath.

The soul hath quickened every part—
   That remnant of a martial brow,

Those ribs that held the mighty heart,
　　That strong arm—strong no longer now.
Spare them, each mouldering relic spare,
　　Of God's own image ; let them rest,
Till not a trace shall speak of where
　　The awful likeness was impressed.

For he was fresher from the hand
　　That formed of earth the human face,
And to the elements did stand
　　In nearer kindred than our race.
In many a flood to madness tossed,
　　In many a storm has been his path ;
He hid him not from heat or frost,
　　But met them, and defied their wrath.

Then they were kind—the forests here,
　　Rivers, and stiller waters, paid
A tribute to the net and spear
　　Of the red ruler of the shade.

Fruits on the woodland branches lay,
　　Roots in the shaded soil below,
The stars looked forth to teach his way,
　　The still earth warned him of the foe.

A noble race ! but they are gone,
　　With their old forests wide and deep,
And we have built our homes upon
　　Fields where their generations sleep.
Their fountains slake our thirst at noon,
　　Upon their fields our harvest waves,
Our lovers woo beneath their moon—
　　Then let us spare at least their graves !

MIDSUMMER.

A SONNET.

A POWER is on the earth and in the air,
From which the vital spirit shrinks afraid,
And shelters him, in nooks of deepest shade,
From the hot steam and from the fiery glare.
Look forth upon the earth—her thousand plants
Are smitten ; even the dark sun-loving maize
Faints in the field beneath the torrid blaze ;
The herd beside the shaded fountain pants ;
For life is driven from all the landscape brown ;

The bird hath sought his tree, the snake his
    den,
The trout floats dead in the hot stream, and
    men
Drop by the sun-stroke in the populous town :
    As if the Day of Fire had dawned, and sent
    Its deadly breath into the firmament.

THE GREEK PARTISAN.

Our free flag is dancing
  In the free mountain air,
And burnished arms are glancing,
  And warriors gathering there !
And fearless is the little train
  Whose gallant bosoms shield it ,
The blood that warms their hearts shall stain
  That banner ere they yield it.
—Each dark eye is fixed on earth,
  And brief each solemn greeting ;
There is no look nor sound of mirth,
  Where those stern men are meeting.

They go to the slaughter,
  To strike the sudden blow,
And pour on earth, like water,
  The best blood of the foe ;
To rush on them from rock and height,
  And clear the narrow valley,
Or fire their camp at dead of night,
  And fly before they rally.
—Chains are round our country pressed,
  And cowards have betrayed her,
And we must make her bleeding breast
  The grave of the invader.

Not till from her fetters
  We raise up Greece again,
And write, in bloody letters,
  That tyranny is slain,—
Oh, not till then the smile shall steal
  Across those darkened faces,
Nor one of all those warriors feel

His children's dear embraces.
—Reap we not the ripened wheat,
Till yonder hosts are flying,
And all their bravest, at our feet,
Like autumn sheaves are lying.

THE TWO GRAVES.

'TIS a bleak wild hill, but green and bright
In the summer warmth and the mid-day light;
There's the hum of the bee and the chirp of the
    wren,
And the dash of the brook from the alder glen;
There's the sound of a bell from the scattered
    flock,
And the shade of the beech lies cool on the
    rock,
And fresh from the west is the free wind's
    breath,—
There is nothing here that speaks of death.

Far yonder, where orchards and gardens lie,
And dwellings cluster, 'tis there men die.
They are born, they die, and are buried near,
Where the populous grave-yard lightens the
            bier ;
For strict and close are the ties that bind
In death the children of human-kind ;
Yea, stricter and closer than those of life,—
'Tis a neighborhood that knows no strife.
They are noiselessly gathered—friend and foe—
To the still and dark assemblies below.
Without a frown or a smile they meet,
Each pale and calm in his winding-sheet ;
In that sullen home of peace and gloom,
Crowded, like guests in a banquet-room.

Yet there are graves in this lonely spot,
Two humble graves, but I meet them not.
I have seen them,—eighteen years are past,
Since I found their place in the brambles last,—

The place where, fifty winters ago,
And aged man in his locks of snow,
And an aged matron, withered with years,
Were solemnly laid !—but not with tears.
For none, who sat by the light of their hearth,
Beheld their coffins covered with earth ;
Their kindred were far, and their children dead,
When the funeral prayer was coldly said.

Two low green hillocks, two small gray stones,
Rose over the place that held their bones ;
But the grassy hillocks are levelled again,
And the keenest eye might search in vain,
'Mong briers, and ferns, and paths of sheep,
For the spot where the aged couple sleep.

Yet well might they lay, beneath the soil
Of this lonely spot, that man of toil,

And trench the strong hard mould with the
        spade,
Where never before a grave was made ;
For he hewed the dark old woods away,
And gave the virgin fields to the day ;
And the gourd and the bean, beside his door,
Bloomed where their flowers ne'er opened be-
            fore ;
And the maize stood up, and the bearded rye
Bent low in the breath of an unknown sky.

'Tis said that when life is ended here,
The spirit is borne to a distant sphere ;
That it visits its earthly home no more,
Nor looks on the haunts it loved before.
But why should the bodiless soul be sent
Far off, to a long, long banishment ?
Talk not of the light and the living green !
It will pine for the dear familiar scene ;

It will yearn, in that strange bright world, to
     behold
The rock and the stream it knew of old.

  'Tis a cruel creed, believe it not !
Death to the good is a milder lot.
They are here,—they are here,—that harmless
     pair,
In the yellow sunshine and flowing air,
In the light cloud-shadows that slowly pass,
In the sounds that rise from the murmuring
     grass.
They sit where their humble cottage stood,
They walk by the waving edge of the wood,
And list to the long accustomed flow
Of the brook that wets the rocks below.
Patient, and peaceful, and passionless,
As seasons on seasons swiftly press,
They watch, and wait, and linger around,
Till the day when their bodies shall leave the
     ground.

THE CONJUNCTION OF JUPITER
AND VENUS.

I WOULD not always reason.   The straight
    path
Wearies us with its never-varying lines,
And we grow melancholy.   I would make
Reason my guide, but she should sometimes sit
Patiently by the way-side, while I traced
The mazes of the pleasant wilderness
Around me.   She should be my counsellor,
But not my tyrant.   For the spirit needs
Impulses from a deeper source than hers,

And there are motions, in the mind of man,
That she must look upon with awe.   I bow
Reverently to her dictates, but not less
Hold to the fair illusions of old time—
Illusions that shed brightness over life,
And glory over nature.   Look, even now,
Where two bright planets in the twilight meet,
Upon the saffron heaven,—the imperial star
Of Jove, and she that from her radiant urn
Pours forth the light of love.   Let me believe,
Awhile, that they are met for ends of good,
Amid the evening glory, to confer
Of men and their affairs, and to shed down
Kind influence.   Lo! they brighten as we gaze,
And shake out softer fires!   The great earth
        feels
The gladness and the quiet of the time.
Meekly the mighty river, that infolds
This mighty city, smooths his front, and far
Glitters and burns even to the rocky base

Of the dark heights that bound him to the
     west ;
And a deep murmur, from the many streets,
Rises like a thanksgiving.   Put we hence
Dark and sad thoughts awhile—there's time for
     them
Hereafter—on the morrow we will meet,
With melancholy looks, to tell our griefs,
And make each other wretched ; this calm hour,
This balmy, blessed evening, we will give
To cheerful hopes and dreams of happy days,
Born of the meeting of those glorious stars.

   Enough of drought has parched the year and
     scared
The land with dread of famine.   Autumn, yet,
Shall make men glad with unexpected fruits.
The dog-star shall shine harmless : genial days
Shall softly glide away into the keen
And wholesome cold of winter ; he that fears

The pestilence, shall gaze on those pure beams,
And breathe, with confidence, the quiet air.

   Emblems of power and beauty ! well may they
Shine brightest on our borders, and withdraw
Towards the great Pacific, marking out
The path of empire. Thus, in our own land,
Ere long, the better Genius of our race,
Having encompassed earth, and tamed its tribes,
Shall sit him down beneath the farthest west,
By the shore of that calm ocean, and look back
On realms made happy.

             Light the nuptial torch,
And say the glad yet solemn rite that knits
The youth and maiden. Happy days to them
That wed this evening !—a long life of love,
And blooming sons and daughters ! Happy they

Born at this hour,—for they shall see an age
Whiter and holier than the past, and go
Late to their graves.   Men shall wear softer
          hearts,
And shudder at the butcheries of war,
As now at other murders.

                         Hapless Greece !
Enough of blood has wet thy rocks, and stained
Thy rivers ; deep enough thy chains have worn
Their links into thy flesh ; the sacrifice
Of thy pure maidens, and thy innocent babes,
And reverend priests, has expiated all
Thy crimes of old.   In yonder mingling lights
There is an omen of good days for thee.
Thou shalt arise from midst the dust and sit
Again among the nations.   Thine own arm
Shall yet redeem thee.   Not in wars like thine
The world takes part.   Be it a strife of kings,
Despot with despot battling for a throne,

And Europe shall be stirred throughout her
      realms,
Nations shall put on harness, and shall fall
Upon each other, and in all their bounds
The wailing of the childless shall not cease.
Thine is a war for liberty, and thou
Must fight it single-handed. The old world
Looks coldly on the murderers of thy race,
And leaves thee to the struggle ; and the new—
I fear me thou couldst tell a shameful tale
Of fraud and lust of gain ;—thy treasury drained,
And Missolonghi fallen. Yet thy wrongs
Shall put new strength into thy heart and hand,
And God and thy good sword shall yet work out,
For thee, a terrible deliverance.

A SUMMER RAMBLE.

The quiet August noon has come,
   A slumberous silence fills the sky,
The fields are still, the woods are dumb,
   In glassy sleep the waters lie.

And mark yon soft white clouds that rest
   Above our vale, a moveless throng ;
The cattle on the mountain's breast
   Enjoy the grateful shadow long.

Oh, how unlike those merry hours,
 In early June, when Earth laughs out,
When the fresh winds make love to flowers,
 And woodlands sing and waters shout.

When in the grass sweet voices talk,
 And strains of tiny music swell
From every moss-cup of the rock,
 From every nameless blossom's bell.

But now a joy too deep for sound,
 A peace no other season knows,
Hushes the heavens and wraps the ground,
 The blessing of supreme repose.

Away ! I will not be, to-day,
 The only slave of toil and care.
Away from desk and dust ! away !
 I'll be as idle as the air.

Beneath the open sky abroad,
　　Among the plants and breathing things,
The sinless, peaceful works of God,
　　I'll share the calm the season brings.

Come, thou, in whose soft eyes I see
　　The gentle meanings of thy heart,
One day amid the woods with me,
　　From men and all their cares apart.

And where, upon the meadow's breast,
　　The shadow of the thicket lies,
The blue wild flowers thou gatherest
　　Shall glow yet deeper near thine eyes.

Come, and when mid the calm profound,
　　I turn, those gentle eyes to seek,
They, like the lovely landscape round,
　　Of innocence and peace shall speak.

Rest here, beneath the unmoving shade,
And on the silent valleys gaze,
Winding and widening, till they fade
In yon soft ring of summer haze.

The village trees their summits rear
Still as its spire, and yonder flock,
At rest in those calm fields, appear
As chiselled from the lifeless rock.

One tranquil mount the scene o'erlooks—
There the hushed winds their sabbath keep,
While a near hum from bees and brooks
Comes faintly like the breath of sleep.

Well may the gazer deem that when,
Worn with the struggle and the strife,
And heart-sick at the wrongs of men,
The good forsakes the scene of life ;

Like this deep quiet that, awhile,
   Lingers the lovely landscape o'er,
Shall be the peace whose holy smile
   Welcomes him to a happier shore.

A SCENE ON THE BANKS OF THE HUDSON.

Cool shades and dews are round my way,
And silence of the early day ;
Mid the dark rocks that watch his bed,
Glitters the mighty Hudson spread,
Unrippled, save by drops that fall
From shrubs that fringe his mountain wall ;
And o'er the clear still water swells
The music of the Sabbath bells.

All, save this little nook of land
Circled with trees, on which I stand ;

All, save that line of hills which lie
Suspended in the mimic sky—
Seems a blue void, above, below,
Through which the white clouds come and go,
And from the green world's farthest steep
I gaze into the airy deep.

Loveliest of lovely things are they,
On earth, that soonest pass away.
The rose that lives its little hour
Is prized beyond the sculptured flower.
Even love, long tried and cherished long,
Becomes more tender and more strong,
At thought of that insatiate grave
From which its yearnings cannot save.

River ! in this still hour thou hast
Too much of heaven on earth to last ;
Nor long may thy still waters lie,
An image of the glorious sky.

Thy fate and mine are not repose,
And, ere another evening close,
Thou to thy tides shalt turn again,
And I to seek the crowd of men.

THE HURRICANE.

Lord of the winds ! I feel thee nigh,
I know thy breath in the burning sky !
And I wait, with a thrill in every vein,
For the coming of the hurricane !

And lo ! on the wing of the heavy gales,
Through the boundless arch of heaven he sails ;
Silent and slow, and terribly strong,
The mighty shadow is borne along,

Like the dark eternity to come ;
While the world below, dismayed and dumb,
Through the calm of the thick hot atmosphere
Looks up at its gloomy folds with fear.

They darken fast ; and the golden blaze
Of the sun is quenched in the lurid haze,
And he sends through the shade a funeral
  ray—
A glare that is neither night nor day,
A beam that touches, with hues of death,
The clouds above and the earth beneath.
To its covert glides the silent bird,
While the hurricane's distant voice is heard,
Uplifted among the mountains round,
And the forests hear and answer the sound.

He is come ! he is come ! do ye not behold
His ample robes on the wind unrolled ?

Giant of air ! we bid thee hail !—
How his gray skirts toss in the whirling gale ;
How his huge and writhing arms are bent,
To clasp the zone of the firmament,
And fold at length, in their dark embrace,
From mountain to mountain the visible space.

Darker—still darker ! the whirlwinds bear
The dust of the plains to the middle air :
And hark to the crashing, long and loud,
Of the chariot of God in the thunder-cloud !
You may trace its path by the flashes that start
From the rapid wheels where'er they dart,
As the fire-bolts leap to the world below,
And flood the skies with a lurid glow.

What roar is that ?—'tis the rain that breaks
In torrents away from the airy lakes,
Heavily poured on the shuddering ground,
And shedding a nameless horror round.

Ah ! well known woods, and mountains, and
     skies,
With the very clouds !—ye are lost to my eyes.
I seek ye vainly, and see in your place
The shadowy tempest that sweeps through space,
A whirling ocean that fills the wall
Of the crystal heaven, and buries all.
And I, cut off from the world, remain
Alone with the terrible hurricane.

WILLIAM TELL.

CHAINS may subdue the feeble spirit, but thee,
   TELL, of the iron heart ! they could not tame !
   For thou wert of the mountains ; they pro-
      claim
The everlasting creed of liberty.
That creed is written on the untrampled snow,
   Thundered by torrents which no power can
      hold,
   Save that of God, when he sends forth his cold,

And breathed by winds that through the free
      heaven blow.
Thou, while thy prison walls were dark around,
  Didst meditate the lesson Nature taught,
  And to thy brief captivity was brought
A vision of thy Switzerland unbound.
  The bitter cup they mingled, strengthened
      thee
  For the great work to set thy country free.

THE HUNTER'S SERENADE.

Thy bower is finished, fairest !
　Fit bower for hunter's bride—
Where old woods overshadow
　The green savanna's side.
I've wandered long, and wandered far,
　And never have I met,
In all this lovely western land,
　A spot so lovely yet.
But I shall think it fairer,
　When thou art come to bless,

With thy sweet smile and silver voice,
    Its silent loveliness.

For thee the wild grape glistens
    On sunny knoll and tree,
The slim papaya ripens
    Its yellow fruit for thee.
For thee the duck, on glassy stream,
    The prairie-fowl shall die,
My rifle for thy feast shall bring
    The wild swan from the sky.
The forest's leaping panther,
    Fierce, beautiful, and fleet,
Shall yield his spotted hide to be
    A carpet for thy feet.

I know, for thou hast told me,
    Thy maiden love of flowers ;
Ah, those that deck thy gardens
    Are pale compared with ours.

When our wide woods and mighty lawns
　　Bloom to the April skies,
The earth has no more gorgeous sight
　　To show to human eyes.
In meadows red with blossoms,
　　All summer long, the bee
Murmurs, and loads his yellow thighs,
　　For thee, my love, and me.

Or wouldst thou gaze at tokens
　　Of ages long ago—
Our old oaks stream with mosses,
　　And sprout with misletoe ;
And mighty vines, like serpents, climb
　　The giant sycamore ;
And trunks, o'erthrown for centuries,
　　Cumber the forest floor ;
And in the great savannas
　　The solitary mound,
Built by the elder world, o'erlooks
　　The loneliness around.

Come, thou hast not forgotten
    Thy pledge and promise quite,
With many blushes murmured,
    Beneath the evening light.
Come, the young violets crowd my door,
    Thy earliest look to win,
And at my silent window-sill
    The jessamine peeps in.
All day the red-bird warbles,
    Upon the mulberry near,
And the night-sparrow trills her song,
    All night, with none to hear.

THE GREEK BOY.

Gone are the glorious Greeks of old,
　　Glorious in mien and mind ;
Their bones are mingled with the mould,
　　Their dust is on the wind ;
The forms they hewed from living stone
Survive the waste of years alone,
And, scattered with their ashes, show
What greatness perished long ago.

Yet fresh the myrtles there—the springs
　　Gush brightly as of yore ;

Flowers blossom from the dust of kings,
    As many an age before.
There nature moulds as nobly now,
As e'er of old, the human brow ;
And copies still the martial form
That braved Platæa's battle storm.

Boy ! thy first looks were taught to seek
    Their heaven in Hellas' skies ;
Her airs have tinged thy dusky cheek,
    Her sunshine lit thine eyes ;
Thine ears have drunk the woodland strains
Heard by old poets, and thy veins
Swell with the blood of demigods,
That slumber in thy country's sods.

Now is thy nation free—though late—
    Thy elder brethren broke—
Broke, ere thy spirit felt its weight,
    The intolerable yoke.

And Greece, decayed, dethroned, doth see
Her youth renewed in such as thee :
A shoot of that old vine that made
The nations silent in its shade.

THE PAST.

Thou unrelenting Past !
Strong are the barriers round thy dark domain,
    And fetters, sure and fast,
Hold all that enter thy unbreathing reign.

    Far in thy realm withdrawn
Old empires sit in sullenness and gloom,
    And glorious ages gone
Lie deep within the shadow of thy womb.

Childhood, with all its mirth,
Youth, Manhood, Age that draws us to the
        ground,
    And last, Man's Life on earth,
Glide to thy dim dominions, and are bound.

Thou hast my better years,
Thou hast my earlier friends—the good—the
        kind,
    Yielded to thee with tears—
The venerable form—the exalted mind.

My spirit yearns to bring
The lost ones back—yearns with desire intense,
    And struggles hard to wring
Thy bolts apart, and pluck thy captives thence

In vain—thy gates deny
All passage save to those who hence depart ;
    Nor to the streaming eye
Thou giv'st them back—nor to the broken heart.

In thine abysses hide
Beauty and excellence unknown––to thee
   Earth's wonder and her pride
Are gathered, as the waters to the sea ;

   Labors of good to man,
Unpublished charity, unbroken faith,––
   Love, that midst grief began,
And grew with years, and faltered not in death

   Full many a mighty name
Lurks in thy depths, unuttered, unrevered ;
   With thee are silent fame,
Forgotten arts, and wisdom disappeared.

   Thine for a space are they––
Yet shalt thou yield thy treasures up at last ;
   Thy gates shall yet give way,
Thy bolts shall fall, inexorable Past !

All that of good and fair
Has gone into thy womb from earliest time,
    Shall then come forth to wear
The glory and the beauty of its prime.

    They have not perished—no !
Kind words, remembered voices once so sweet,
    Smiles, radiant long ago,
And features, the great soul's apparent seat.

All shall come back, each tie
Of pure affection shall be knit again ;
    Alone shall Evil die,
And Sorrow dwell a prisoner in thy reign.

    And then shall I behold
Him, by whose kind paternal side I sprung,
    And her, who, still and cold,
Fills the next grave—the beautiful and young.

NOTES.

NOTES TO VOL. I.

Page 1.

POEM OF THE AGES.

In this poem, written and first printed in the year 1821, the author has endeavored, from a survey of the past ages of the world, and of the successive advances of mankind in knowledge, virtue, and happiness, to justify and confirm the hopes of the philanthropist for the future destinies of the human race.

Page 57.

THE BURIAL-PLACE.

The first half of this fragment may seem to the reader borrowed from the essay on Rural Funerals in the fourth number of the Sketch-Book.   The lines were, however, written more than a year before that number appeared.   The poem, unfinished as it is, would not have been admitted into this collection, had not the author been unwilling to lose what had the honor of resembling so beautiful a composition.

Page 82.

THE MASSACRE AT SCIO.

This poem, written about the time of the horrible butchery of the Sciotes by the Turks, in 1824, has been more fortunate than most poetical predictions.   The independence of the Greek nation, which it foretold, has come to pass, and the massacre, by inspiring a deeper detestation of their oppressors, did much to promote that event.

Page 84.

Her maiden veil, her own black hair, &c.

" The unmarried females have a modest falling down of the hair over the eyes."—ELIOT.

Page 129.

MONUMENT MOUNTAIN.

The mountain called by this name, is a remarkable precipice in Great Barrington, overlooking the rich and picturesque valley of the Housatonic, in the western part of Massachusetts. At the southern extremity is, or was a few years since, a conical pile of small stones, erected, according to the tradition of the surrounding country, by the Indians, in memory of a woman of the Stockbridge tribe, who killed herself by leaping from the edge of the precipice. Until within few years past, small parties of that tribe used to arrive from their settlement in the western part of the State of New York, on visits to Stockbridge, the place of their nativity and former residence. A young woman belonging to one of these parties related, to a friend of the author, the story on which the poem of Monument Mountain is founded. An Indian girl had formed an attachment for her cousin, which, according to the customs of the tribe, was unlawful. She was, in consequence, seized with a deep melancholy, and resolved to destroy herself. In company with a female friend, she repaired to the mountain,

decked out for the occasion in all her ornaments, and,
after passing the day on the summit in singing with her
companion the traditional songs of her nation, she threw
herself headlong from the rock, and was killed.

Page 156.

THE MURDERED TRAVELLER.

Some years since, in the month of May, the remains
of a human body, partly devoured by wild animals, were
found in a woody ravine, near a solitary road passing be-
tween the mountains west of the village of Stockbridge.
It was supposed that the person came to his death by
violence, but no traces could be discovered of his mur-
derers. It was only recollected that one evening, in the
course of the previous winter, a traveller had stopped at
an inn in the village of West Stockbridge; that he had
inquired the way to Stockbridge; and that, in paying
the innkeeper for something he had ordered, it appeared
that he had a considerable sum of money in his posses-
sion. Two ill-looking men were present, and went out
about the same time that the traveller proceeded on his

journey. During the winter, also, two men of shabby appearance, but plentifully supplied with money, had lingered for awhile about the village of Stockbridge. Several years afterward, a criminal, about to be executed for a capital offence in Canada, confessed that he had been concerned in murdering a traveller in Stockbridge for the sake of his money. Nothing was ever discovered respecting the name or residence of the person murdered.

Page 232.

Chained in the market-place he stood, &c.

The story of the African Chief, related in this ballad, may be found in the African Repository for April, 1825. The subject of it was a warrior of majestic stature, the brother of Yarradee, king of the Solima nation. He had been taken in battle, and was brought in chains for sale to the Rio Pongas, where he was exhibited in the market-place, his ankles still adorned with the massy rings of gold which he wore when captured. The refusal of his captor to listen to his offers of ransom drove him mad, and he died a maniac.

Page 256.

THE CONJUNCTION OF JUPITER AND VENUS.

This conjunction was said in the common calendars to have taken place on the 2d of August, 1826. This, I believe, was an error, but the apparent approach of the planets was sufficiently near for poetical purposes.

Page 270.

THE HURRICANE.

This poem is nearly a translation from one by José Maria de Heredia, a native of the Island of Cuba, who published at New York, about the year 1824, a volume of poems in the Spanish language.

Page 274.

WILLIAM TELL.

Neither this, nor any of the other sonnets in the collection, with the exception of the one from the Portuguese, is framed according to the legitimate Italian model, which, in the author's opinion, possesses no peculiar beauty for an ear accustomed only to the metrical forms of our own language. The sonnets in this collection are rather poems in fourteen lines than sonnets.

Page 277.

The slim papaya ripens, &c.

Papaya—papaw, custard-apple. Flint, in his excellent work on the Geography and History of the Western States, thus describes this tree and its fruit:

" A papaw shrub, hanging full of fruits, of a size and weight so disproportioned to the stem, and from under long and rich-looking leaves, of the same yellow with the ripened fruit, and of an African luxuriance of growth, is to us one of the richest spectacles that we have ever contemplated in the array of the woods. The fruit contains from two to six seeds like those of the tamarind, except that they are double the size. The pulp of the fruit resembles egg-custard in consistence and appearance. It has the same creamy feeling in the mouth, and unites the taste of eggs, cream, sugar, and spice. It is a natural custard, too luscious for the relish of most people."

Chateaubriand, in his Travels, speaks disparagingly or the fruit of the papaw; but on the authority of Mr. Flint, who must know more of the matter, I have ventured to make my western lover enumerate it among the delicacies of the wilderness.